Ultimate bass boats

by Monte Burch

Stoeger Publishing Company, Accokeek, Maryland

Stoeger Publishing
Great Outdoor Books Since 1925

STOEGER PUBLISHING COMPANY
is a division of Benelli U.S.A.

Benelli U.S.A.
Vice President and General Manager: Stephen Otway
Director of Brand Marketing and Communications:
  Stephen McKelvain

Stoeger Publishing Company
President: Jeffrey Reh
Publisher: Jay Langston
Managing Editor: Harris J. Andrews
Art Director: Cynthia T. Richardson
Photography Director: Alex Bowers
Imaging Specialist: William Graves
Copy Editor: Kate Baird
Publishing Assistant: Christine Lawton
Technical Illustration: William Graves

Published by Stoeger Publishing Company
17603 Indian Head Highway, Suite 200
Accokeek, Maryland 20607

BK6470
ISBN:0-88317-236-4
Library of Congress Control Number: 2002105918

Manufactured in the United States of America
Distributed to the book trade and
to the sporting goods trade by:
Stoeger Industries
17603 Indian Head HIghway, Suite 200
Accokeek, Maryland 20607
301 283-6300   Fax: 301-283-6300
www.stoegerindustries.com

OTHER PUBLICATIONS:
Shooter's Bible 2003 - 94th Edition
  The World's Standard Firearms
    Reference Book
Gun Trader's Guide - 25th Edition
  Complete Fully Illustrated
    Guide to Modern Firearms
    with Current Market Values
Bassing Bible 2003
  The Ultimate Bass Fishing
    Reference Guide

Hunting & Shooting
  Hounds of the World
  The Turkey Hunter's Tool Kit:
    Shooting Savvy
  Complete Book of Whitetail Hunting
  Hunting and Shooting with
    the Modern Bow
  The Ultimate in Rifle Accuracy
  Advanced Black Powder Hunting
  Labrador Retrievers
  Hunting America's Wild Turkey
  Taxidermy Guide
  Cowboy Action Shooting
  Great Shooters of the World

Collecting Books
  Sporting Collectibles
  The Working Folding Knife
  The Lore of Spices

Firearms
  Antique Guns
  P-38 Automatic Pistol
  The Walther Handgun Story
  Complete Guide to Compact Handguns
  Complete Guide to Service Handguns
  America's Great Gunmakers
  Firearms Disassembly with Exploded Views
  Rifle Guide
  Gunsmithing at Home
  The Book of the Twenty-Two
  Complete Guide to Modern Rifles
  Complete Guide to Classic Rifles
  Legendary Sporting Rifles
  FN Browning Armorer to the World
  Modern Beretta Firearms
  How to Buy & Sell Used Guns
  Heckler & Koch: Armorers of the Free
    World
  Spanish Handguns

Reloading
  The Handloader's Manual of Cartridge
    Conversions
  Modern Sporting Rifle Cartridges
  Complete Reloading Guide

Fishing
  Ultimate Bass Boats
  The Flytier's Companion
  Deceiving Trout
  The Complete Book of Trout Fishing
  The Complete Book of Flyfishing
  Peter Dean's Guide to Fly-Tying
  The Flytier's Manual
  Flytier's Master Class
  Handbook of Fly Tying
  The Fly Fisherman's Entomological
    Pattern Book
  Fiberglass Rod Making
  To Rise a Trout

Motorcycles & Trucks
  The Legend of Harley-Davidson
  The Legend of the Indian
  Best of Harley-Davidson
  Classic Bikes
  Great Trucks
  4X4 Vehicles

Cooking Game
  Fish & Shellfish Care & Cookery
  Game Cookbook
  Dress 'Em Out
  Wild about Venison
  Wild about Game Birds

PHOTOGRAPHY CREDITS
Cover: Courtesy Ranger Boats; 4: Jan Finger/Windigo
  Images; 16 *(bottom)*: John Tiger; 22: Courtesy
  Yamaha; 34: Courtesy Mercury Marine; 58:
  Courtesy DieHard; 122: Courtesy Nitro; 123 *(left)*:
  Courtesy Ranger Boats; 123(bottom): Bassmaster;
  124 *(top)*: Courtesy Triton Boats; 124 *(bottom)*:
  Courtesy Skeeter Boats; 125 *(left)*: Courtesy Triton
  Boats; 125 *(right)*: Bassmaster; 126 *(left)*: Courtesy
  Nitro; 126 *(right)*: Bassmaster

Contents

"The Black Bass is our chief object of pursuit —
his capture is our dearest triumph — his captive form our proudest trophy.
When word first comes, in June, that the Black Bass bites in our river,
what a stir there is among our anglers!
— what questioning as to the when, and the where, and by whom,
and with what bait, and size! — what an anxious inquiry after big minnows!
— what a raking and scraping of pond-holes for soft lobsters!
— what a watching of the skies! — and if there be no wind,
or a zephyr from the south or west, what bright and hopeful faces!
... And why the commotion? Because this is the very prince of game-fishes.
His capture is a less easy task, and involves, or is supposed to involve more science,
and to be truer proof of the merit as an angler,
than any other tenant of our crystal waters."

Frank Forrester's Fish and Fishing of the United States, 1849

About the Author

One of the nation's most widely read and prolific authors, Monte Burch is a nationally recognized authority on hunting, fishing, boating, camping and natural history. He has written extensively on subjects ranging from do-it-yourself woodworking and construction projects to hunting and consumer affairs. During his forty-year career Monte Burch has worked as a building contractor, newspaper and studio photographer, freelance writer, and editor, and was also a former editor for Kansas City-based *Workbench Magazine*. He even created a nationally syndicated comic strip, the "Good Earth Almanac."

Burch is the author of more than sixty books and his titles include Monte Burch's *Pole Building Projects*, *Building Small Barns*, *Modern Waterfowl Hunting*, *Gun Care* and *Repair, Field Dressing and Butchering Deer*, and *The Field & Stream All-Terrain Vehicle Handbook*. He has also written *How to Build Small Barns & Outbuildings*, which was voted first-place book winner in the 1993 Stanley National Home and Workshop Writers Association writing contest. Many of his articles have been featured in *Popular Science* and various how-to and outdoor publications.

Monte Burch is a member of the Outdoor Writers Association of America, Great Lakes Outdoor Writers, Southeast Outdoor Writers Association, and National Association of Home and Workshop Writers. Together with his wife, Joan, Burch operates a book-publishing house called Outdoor World Press, Inc. He lives in Humansville, Missouri.

Rigging the Ultimate Sportsman's Boat

I f you're looking for a boat to handle a variety of fishing and hunting chores, the Ultimate Sportsman's Boat may fit your needs. A no-nonsense "working" boat that can handle a number of both fishing or hunting chores, the Ultimate Sportsman's Boat begins as an economical but extremely sturdy, Tunnel Hull 16-foot Alumacraft All-Welded Johnboat. Although the plan here illustrates rigging that particular model, the same idea can be used to rig other sizes of boats by adapting the plan to suit.

The Alumacraft 16-footer weighs 300 pounds and has a beam of 74 inches. The boat has a five-person, or B.I.A., capacity of 1,100 pounds and is rated for up to 35 horsepower with tiller steer and 50 horsepower with center console. The boat is first outfitted with wooden decks, carpeting, pedestal seats and other amenities, turning it into the "ultimate" boat for fishing chores ranging from casting for bass to trolling for walleye, bobber fishing for crappie, or even nighttime "cat" hunting.

We chose a tiller steer model for economy and less weight, but also so we could design the interior to suit more fishing and hunting needs. Consoles take up space and create problems for a duck boat. The tiller steer also provides easier and more precise trolling for walleye and other panfish.

The Alumacraft 1650AW model boat is available with an optional center seat/livewell, but we chose to design and build a divided, double livewell system so that the boat could be used for tournament angling with two anglers, or so one livewell could be used for live bait and the other for fish, for instance when walleye angling. The double livewells offer a walk-through so you don't have to step over a seat. The livewells consist of drop-in Tempress plastic liner boxes with Tempress hatches, a simple way to add livewells. Mayfair pumps and Flow-Rite 3-position controls provide optimum livewell performance even for the demands of tournament angling.

Two Moeller high-quality seats with snap-off upholstery and removable pedestals allow for sit-down trolling or casting. Seat height is changed by removing or changing pedestal heights. A Minn Kota All-Terrain bow-mount trolling motor is mounted in place for bow casting. We designed a quick-release wooden mount, however, the Minn Kota PowerDrive Quick-Release mount for use with the PowerDrive and AutoPilot bow-mount units is also available, and easier to use. Both allow the motor to be easily removed for duck boat use. Bow and stern LCR's provide plenty of underwater information. The floor, decks, and livewells are carpeted using a replacement carpet kit from BassPro Shops Marine. Carpeting adds a bit more weight, but makes the floor less slick, the boat quieter, and finishes off the interior.

The tunnel hull design provides for extremely shallow water usage, making the boat perfect for fishing rivers with shoals and bars as well as weedy shallow bays. The boat can even be used in shallow saltwater situations, and provides excellent performance for waterfowling in shallow bays, flats and marshes.

First, trailer the boat and install the motor as per the manufacturer's instructions, or, you may prefer to have your dealer do these chores.

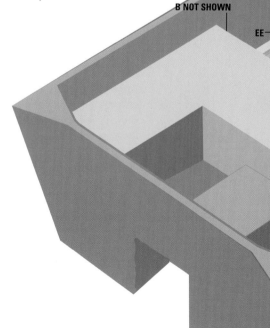

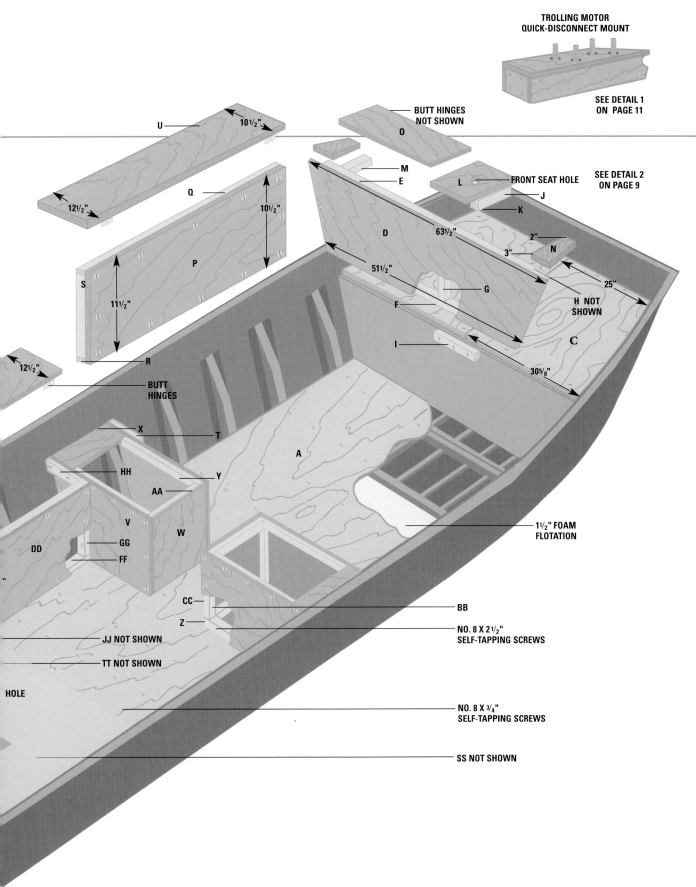

TROLLING MOTOR
QUICK-DISCONNECT MOUNT

SEE DETAIL 1
ON PAGE 11

BUTT HINGES
NOT SHOWN

U

10½"

O

M
E

SEE DETAIL 2
ON PAGE 9

L

FRONT SEAT HOLE

J

Q

12½"

10½"

K

P

D

63½"

2"

N

3"

S

51½"

G

25"

11½"

F

H NOT
SHOWN

I

C

R

30⅝"

12½"

BUTT
HINGES

X

T

HH

Y

AA

V

W

1½" FOAM
FLOTATION

DD

GG

FF

CC

BB

Z

NO. 8 X 2½"
SELF-TAPPING SCREWS

JJ NOT SHOWN

TT NOT SHOWN

HOLE

NO. 8 X ¾"
SELF-TAPPING SCREWS

SS NOT SHOWN

MATERIALS LIST–
FISHING BOAT INTERIOR

Note: All plywood should be pressure-treated or marine grade.

FLOOR

A   Floor, ½" plywood, 46½" x 92½", 1 req'd.
B   Floor, ½" plywood, 8½" x 46½", 1 req'd.

FRONT DECK ASSEMBLY

C   Deck, ½" plywood, 30⅝" x 41", cut to fit, 2 req'd.
D   Front Deck Support, ½" plywood, 13" x 63½", 1 req'd.
E   Top Front Deck Brace, 1½" x 1½" x 60", 1 req'd.
F   Bottom Front Deck Brace, 1½" x 1½" x 46½", cut to fit, 1 req'd.
G   Center Front Deck Brace, 1½" x 1½" x 10", 1 req'd.
H   Side Front Deck Braces, 1½" x 1½" x 11½", cut to fit, 2 req'd.
I   Front Seat Support Cleat, 1½" x 1½" x 8½", 1 req'd.
J   Front Seat Under Support, ¾" treated solid stock, 9" x 11½", 1 req'd.
K   Front Seat Side Support Cleats, 1½" x 1½" x 7", 2 req'd.
L   Front Seat Deck, ½" plywood, 10" x 11", 1 req'd.
M   Front Side Deck Support Cleats, ¾" x 1½" x 7", 2 req'd.
N   Front Side Deck, ½" plywood, 3" x 11", 2 req'd.
O   Front Lids, ½" plywood, 10½" x 24", 2 req'd.

FRONT COMPARTMENT ASSEMBLY

P   Front Compartment Side Panels, ½" plywood, 11½" x 32", cut to fit, 2 req'd.
Q   Upper Front Compartment Side Cleats, ¾" x 1½" x 32", 2 req'd.
R   Lower Front Compartment Side Cleats, ¾" x 1½" x 32", 2 req'd.
S   Front Compartment Vertical Cleats:
     Front ¾" x 1½" x 9", 2 req'd.
     Rear   ¾" x 1½" x 10", 2 req'd.
T   Front Compartment Lid Supports:
     Front ½" x 1½" x 8½", 2 req'd.
     Rear   ½" x 1½" x 10", 2 req'd.
U   Front Compartment Lids, ½" plywood, 12½" x 31", 2 req'd.

LIVEWELL ASSEMBLY

V   Livewell Sides, ½" plywood, 12" x 29", 4 req'd.
W   Livewell Ends, ½" plywood, 12" x 14", 2 req'd.
X   Livewell Tops, ¾" treated solid stock, 6" x 14", 2 req'd.
Y   Livewell Upper Side Cleats, ¾" x 1½" x 22¼", 4 req'd.
Z   Livewell Lower Side Cleats, ¾" x 1½" x 20", 4 req'd.
AA   Livewell Upper Horizontal Cleats, ¾" x 1½" x 14", 2 req'd.
BB   Livewell Lower Horizontal Cleats, ¾" x 1½ "x 12½", 2 req'd.
CC   Livewell Vertical Cleats, ¾" x 1½" x 9", 4 req'd.

REAR COMPARTMENT ASSEMBLY

DD   Rear Compartment Sides, ½" plywood, 12" x 43", 2 req'd.
EE   Upper Rear Compartment Horizontal Cleats, ¾" x 1½" x 43", 2 req'd.
FF   Lower Rear Compartment Horizontal Cleats, ¾" x 1½" x 43", 2 req'd.
GG   Vertical Rear Compartment Cleats:
     Front ¾" x 1½" x 10", 2 req'd.
     Rear   ¾" x 1½" x 9", 2 req'd.
HH   Rear Compartment Lid Supports:
     Front ¾" x 1½" x 10", 2 req'd.
     Rear   ¾" x 1½" x 8½", 2 req'd.
II   Rear Compartment Lids, ½" plywood, 12½" x 42", 2 req'd.
JJ   Rear Deck Hole Cover Plate, ¼" plywood, 10" x 10", 1 req'd.

TROLLING MOTOR MOUNT ASSEMBLY

KK   Trolling Motor Mount Bottom, ¾" treated solid stock, 7" x 12¼", cut to fit, 1 req'd.
LL   Trolling Motor Mount Inside Side, ¾" treated solid stock, 3½" x 14¼", 1 req'd.
MM   Trolling Motor Mount Inside Side, ¾" treated solid stock, 3½" x 19¼", 1 req'd.
NN   Trolling Motor Mount Inside Top, ¾" treated solid stock, 7" x 19¼", 1 req'd.
OO   Trolling Motor Mount Outside Side, ½" plywood, 5" x 15", 1 req'd.
PP   Trolling Motor Mount Outside Side, ½" plywood, 5" x 20", 1 req'd.
QQ   Trolling Motor Mount Outside Top, ½" plywood, 8" x 20", cut to fit, 1 req'd.
RR   End Cap, ¾" treated solid stock, 5" x 7", 1 req'd.
SS   Rear Floor Support, 1½" x 1½" x 12", cut to fit, 2 req'd.
TT   Rear Under Seat Support, ½" plywood, 7" x 7", 2 req'd.

ALSO REQUIRED:

Foam Flotation, 1½" x 4' x 8', 1 sheet req'd.
Self-Tapping Screws, No. 8 x ¾", 6 dozen req'd.
Self-Tapping Screws, No. 8 x 1½ ", 4 dozen req'd.
Self-Tapping Screws, No. 8 x 2½ ", 2 dozen req'd.
Seat Bolts, Lock Washers, Washers and Nuts, ¼" x 3", 1 dozen each req'd.
Butt Hinges, 1½", 6 pairs req'd.
Plywood Sealer, Wood Sealer, or Exterior House Paint, any color.
BassPro Shops Boat Carpet Replacement Kit, brown, 8' x 21', 1 req'd.
Trolling Motor Mounting Bolts, ⅜" x 2¾", 4 to 6 req'd.
Trolling Motor Mounting Washers, 3 req'd. for each bolt.
Trolling Motor Mounting Nuts, 2 req'd. for each bolt.
Trolling Motor Mounting Lock Washers, 1 req'd. for each bolt.

CONSTRUCTION

Construction of both the interior rigging of the fishing version as well as the add-on waterfowl blind is not difficult, although it does take some woodworking skills and a few tools. It will also take a fair amount of time – about four weekends for the average home woodworker to complete the fishing version.

Tools Required

The project can be constructed with basic hand tools – a hammer, handsaw, c-clamps, tape measure, and square. You'll also need a portable electric saw with ripping guide, saber saw with both plywood- and metal-cutting blades, portable electric drill, a set of drill bits, drill-screwdriver heads, and a hole saw kit. If the power drill is a rechargeable model, so much the better, due to its convenience. If you have two drills, the chore of fastening will go more quickly, since almost all construction consists of self-tapping screws driven in pre-bored holes.

Bottom Construction

Construction starts with the boat bottom. Cut pieces of $1\frac{1}{2}$" foam flotation to fit between each of the cross ribs of the boat bottom. Then rip a piece of $\frac{1}{2}$" treated plywood (A) to the correct width, and cut to length. Plywood must be cut to length so the edge will anchor in the middle of the last rear cross rib of the boat. Position this down flat on the foam and cross ribs. Align the front edge of the plywood with the rear edge of the existing metal deck of the boat, and anchor in place with self-tapping screws through holes bored through the plywood and the tops of the metal cross ribs of the boat. A full-length 8' sheet of plywood won't cover the bottom. A small section (B) must be cut to cover the rear of the boat. This section is also anchored in place with self-tapping screws through the plywood and into the rib. *Note: Rear floor supports (SS) are first anchored to the front bottom edge of the rear deck to help support the floor, as there is no bottom cross rib in that location.*

Carpeting

A carpet replacement kit is used to carpet the interior of the boat. The bottom is carpeted before the remaining compartments are installed. The best tactic is to carpet the compartments before they are installed. Before installation of the carpet, the wooden surfaces must be sealed to allow the carpet adhesive to adhere properly. This can be done with wood sealer, or exterior latex house paint. The latter is the most economical. Because all surfaces will be carpeted and the color won't show, you can use any exterior house paint for the chore. *Note: All wood surfaces to be carpeted must first be sealed with the wood sealer or exterior latex house paint.*

Front Deck Assembly

The front deck consists of two pieces of plywood over the existing metal deck with an extension to provide more front deck space and support for the pedestal seat. First step is to cut the two front plywood pieces (C) to shape. *Note: These pieces are tapered to fit the tapered front bow and they don't cover the entire deck.*

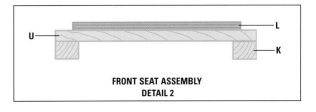

**FRONT SEAT ASSEMBLY
DETAIL 2**

Leave 1" of metal edge for anchoring the extension deck and seat support, as well as supporting the front compartment lids. Anchor the two halves in place on the metal deck with self-tapping screws. Paint to seal the wood, then install carpeting.

Cut the front seat support (I) and fasten in place to the center rear edge of the metal deck. Cut the front deck support (D) to size from plywood. In order to get both side angles properly cut, measure the center of the top and mark across the piece with a square. Then measure from the bottom center mark to each side for the location of the angled side cuts. Rip 2x4s into $1\frac{1}{2}$" x $1\frac{1}{2}$" pieces using a ripping guide with the portable electric saw. Cut the top front deck brace (E), the bottom front deck brace (F), center front deck brace (G), and side front deck braces (H) to length and at the proper angles from the ripped strips. Anchor to the back of the front deck support with self-tapping screws through the plywood into the strips. *Note: The support braces are set back in on both sides so the plywood piece overlaps the back edge of the front side ribs of the boat. This allows you to anchor the plywood solidly to the rib sides with self-tapping screws.* Before installing, paint to seal, and carpet the plywood side. Then anchor in place through the side edges into the side boat ribs. Also, anchor securely through the floor and into the metal rib of the floor with self-tapping screws.

Front Seat Assembly

The front pedestal seat is positioned behind the existing metal deck on a center seat support assembly. This assembly is constructed by first cutting the front seat deck (L) to the correct size. Cut the front seat undersupport (J) to size and fasten the upper piece over it with self-tapping screws. *Note: It does not extend full length front and back, but does extend past the side edges to provide support for the deck lids. This allows the front seat deck to fit down flush on the metal deck and edge of the front deck support and brace.* Bore the hole for the seat pedestal base. This can be bored with a portable electric drill and hole cutters. Cut the two front seat side support cleats (K) and anchor them to the underside of the undersupport (J). With the assembly completed, anchor in place with self-tapping screws through the front edge into the metal deck edge and with screws through the rear edge into the top front deck support. Anchor the ends of the front seat support cleats with screws through them into the center front support cleat, and from the rear of the front deck support into the ends of the front seat side support cleats. Paint and carpet.

Cut the front side deck support cleats (M), then cut the front side deck pieces (N). Fasten the cleats to the underside of the deck pieces with ¾ of an inch protruding toward the compartment opening, then fasten these assemblies in place with self-tapping screws. Paint and carpet. Then cut the front lids (O) and paint and carpet. *Note: All lids are carpeted around the edges and folded over the back.* Once carpeted, hinge in place with butt hinges on the front edge of the lids and the back edge of the front deck.

Front Pedestal Seat

Install the purchased seat pedestal by positioning in place down on the carpeted deck. Bore holes for the holding bolts, and anchor in place with bolts down through the pedestal, through the seat assembly. Anchor in place with washers, lock washers, and nuts.

Livewell Compartments

Cut the livewell sides (V), ends (W), and tops (X) to size. Then cut the livewell inner cleats (Y, Z, AA, BB, and CC) to the correct size. Assemble the livewell compartments with self-tapping screws through the plywood into the inner cleats. Cut notches at the back corner of each livewell for running hoses and wiring. Paint and carpet the compartments. Anchor the livewell compartments to the floor using self-tapping screws through the floor and into the ribs, as well as through the sides of the livewells into the side ribs.

Front Compartments

Cut the front compartment side panels (P) to size. *Note: Panels are tapered with the front lower than the rear.* Cut the front compartment cleats (Q, R, and S) to size and assemble the front compartment sides. Paint and carpet the side panels, then anchor in place with screws through the front compartment cleats and into plywood deck support. Anchor the rear of the front compartment sides in place with screws through from the rear cleats of the front compartment sides and into the livewell compartment sides. Finally, anchor the bottom cleats with screws through

them, through the floor, and into the bottom boat ribs. Cut the front compartment lid supports (T). *Note: There are two different sizes for each front compartment.* It's a good idea to rough-cut all these pieces, hold them in place, and do the final marking and fitting. Anchor one to the inside edge of the front deck, and one in the inside at the rear (livewell side) and finish with the top edges. Then cut the front compartment lids (U) to size. *Note: Again, they are tapered from front to back.* Carpet and hinge in place. *Note: Cloth straps are used at the back edges of the compartment lids to open them, or you can add locking compartment hardware, if you prefer.*

Rear Compartments

The rear compartments are constructed in the same manner, carpeted and anchored in place. Then the compartment lids are cut, carpeted, and hinged to the rear compartments.

Trolling Motor Mount

The trolling motor mount assembly is constructed to position a foot-controlled bow-mount trolling motor flush with the top edge of the bow gunwale. It is also designed to provide a quick-mount system that allows you to remove the trolling motor when the boat is used as a waterfowl blind, providing more bow space for decoys, dog, etc.

First, make a pattern from the squared drawing shown. This will be the shape of the ends of the side pieces that fit against the front gunwale of the boat. Cut the bottom (KK) from ¾" treated solid wood, then cut the inside side pieces (LL and MM) from ¾" treated solid wood. Fasten the bottom to the sides with countersunk screws through the bottom into the bottom edges of the sides. Anchor the bottom/inside side assembly in place on the carpeted deck with self-tapping wood screws that protrude through the wooden deck into the metal deck. Make sure you use plenty of screws to anchor the assembly firmly in place. Cut the outside sides (OO and PP) to the correct shape and size, and anchor to the inside sides and bottom with countersunk wood screws. Then cut the inside top (NN) and anchor it in place with countersunk wood screws down into the top edges of the inside sides. Finally, cut the outside top (QQ) and anchor it in place with countersunk wood screws down into the top edges of the inside sides. Place the trolling motor bracket in position and mark it for mounting bolts, then bore holes for the holding bolts. Countersink the top piece and use bolts with washers up from the bottom, then use washers and nuts in the countersunk holes to permanently anchor the bolts in place.

To install the trolling motor, slide the bracket down over the bolts adding additional washers and nuts. Last step after installation of the trolling motor is to cut the end cap (RR), carpet, and install the outside sides and top with self-tapping screws.

Rear Deck
The rear deck is not covered with plywood. The seat pedestal mounts directly to the metal deck. First, locate the position of the seat pedestal, then use a hole saw and portable electric drill to cut the pedestal extension hole. Position the pedestal in place, mark for the bolt holding holes, and bore them. The rear deck is

filled with foam flotation, and you'll need to be able to get to the underside of the metal deck to properly anchor the seat in place. This is done by cutting an entrance hole in the front of the rear deck upright. First, bore starting holes, then use a saber saw and metal-cutting blade to make an 8" cutout. Using a long, sharp knife, cut away the foam in the general area of the seat so you can reach in and tighten the nuts on the seat-holding bolts. To add additional strength to the seat assembly, cut ½" plywood under-seat supports (TT) to fit beneath the metal deck. *Note: TT is doubled for extra strength.* Bore the pedestal extension hole and bolt holes as well.

Carpet the rear deck and down the front upright deck support. Install the seat pedestal, placing the plywood supports underneath the deck and anchoring the pedestal and under deck supports with bolts, washers, lock washers, and nuts.

Use a saber saw to cut a round rear deck hole cover plate (JJ) from ¼" plywood. Carpet, then anchor this in place with self-tapping screws.

Plumbing and Wiring
A Mayfair bilge pump is anchored to the bottom rib at the back on the right side of the tunnel portion of the stern. A 1" hole is cut with a hole-saw in the upper edge of the rear side near the gunwale, a fitting installed, and the pump hose run to the fitting and pump. The pump switch is

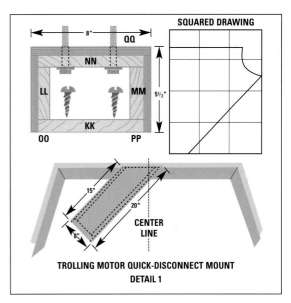

TROLLING MOTOR QUICK-DISCONNECT MOUNT DETAIL 1

placed on the right rear compartment supports. The livewells are constructed by first cutting an opening in the lower rear corner of the drop-in plastic boxes. Fittings are installed, and the pumps and valves positioned and anchored to the inside of the rear compartment sides. The hoses are then installed and the switches are placed on the outside of the rear compartment sides within easy reach. Wires from the bilge and livewell pump switches are run to the rear battery.

The rear deck is finished by adding a depthfinder and an anchor in the left side and rod holders to the right side.

A depthfinder can be positioned on the front deck with the transducer placed on the trolling motor. A small, plastic-enclosed connecting block is placed in a convenient location on the front deck so wiring from the trolling motor and LCR can be easily disconnected. Wiring for this assembly is run from the block to the front trolling motor battery in the center of the front deck compartment.

Chapter 1

History of the Bass Boat

Bass boats began in a garage in Marshall, Texas, in 1948 when Holmes Thurmond, race boat driver and avid angler contructed the first Skeeter.

The history of the bass boat began in 1948 in a garage in Marshall, Texas. Holmes Thurmond dreamed of building a boat for the avid fisherman. A bass angler at heart, he was also an engineer and champion boat racer. With his knowledge of how to design a boat for speed and stability, coupled with a desire for a boat that would make fishing more enjoyable, Thurmond designed and built the world's first bass boat – the Skeeter.

Thurmond's grandson, Butch, recalls growing up with his grandfather and the Skeeter boat. "Grandpa was a boat racer who loved to fish," said Butch. "The original hull was built for speed based on his racing experience. Where we lived was always windy, and Grandpa got tired of the boat being pushed around by the wind. The name Skeeter came from their long, needle-shaped bows."

In the 1950s fiberglass was first used in the boats' construction and by the mid-60s, anglers were demanding bigger boats with increased horsepower and improved handling. Skeeter responded with the Hawk Series of tri-hulls. In 1975 Skeeter's engineers developed the Wrangler, the first V-bottom bass boat.

The evolution of bass boats was greatly influenced by one man — Forrest L. Wood. Together with bass tournament founder, Ray Scott, Forrest helped pioneer the sport of competitive bass fishing. He personally fished the B.A.S.S. circuit, qualifying for two Bassmaster's Classic Events, and went on to become the foremost innovator in bass boat design and safety.

It began in 1968, when Wood founded the Ranger Boat Company. Born to farm and ranch life in a small Arkansas town, Forrest and Nina Wood

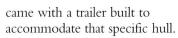

The first Tracker aluminum bass boat hit the market in 1978, setting a trend in packaging boats with everything needed to go fishing. Shown is the author with one of the earlier models of Tracker boats.

were no strangers to hard work. A former fishing guide and excellent fisherman, Forrest brought innovation to the simple bass boats of the day.

Forrest was the first designer to use heavy gauge wire to minimize current loss to the trolling motor and he designed the first aerated livewells to protect fish for live release. His innovations in flotation systems encouraged the U.S. Coast Guard to adopt safety standards that continue to save lives today.

At about the same time Earl Bentz was tearing up the boat racing circuit on the Mercury Racing Team. In the late 70s he experimented with kevlar to produce strong, lightweight, tri-hull bass boats featuring a high-performance pad – the Hydra-Sports. Bentz founded Stratos Boats, creating the VT Rocket Tunnel hull in conjunction with STV Race Boats founder, Roarke Summerford. The Rocket Tunnel hull was pat-

terned after the Model-VP, one of Summerford's most advanced racing hull designs. Paul Allison, a top contender in the boat racing circuit, was also instrumental in introducing high performance bass boats with his Allison Craft line.

A major innovator in bass boat development was John L. Morris of Bass Pro Shops and Tracker Marine. When Johnny fished professional bass tournaments in the 1970s, the business of buying a boat was complicated at best and John turned his attention to simplifying the way American anglers bought boats.

In 1978 Morris produced the first "package" boat, the Bass Tracker. For the first time a manufacturer had taken all of the guesswork out of buying a fully rigged boat. Bass Tracker offered an innovative hull with an outboard matched to optimize performance and the rig

came with a trailer built to accommodate that specific hull.

In the mid-80s the Xpress Hyper Lift hull heralded the introduction of high-performance aluminum bass boats. The addition of a high-performance pad created an aluminum boat that could easily run with the big fiberglass boys.

As hulls became faster, the demand for greater horsepower increased and the race was on. Now 250- and even 300-horsepower engines are common on bass boats. The development of direct fuel injection and big-bore four-stroke motors has played a vital role in bass boat performance. In addition to engine refinements has come amazing advances in sonar and GPS technology.

For the future? Great strides are being made in high-tech materials and boat building techniques and the sky is the limit for electronics and engine technology.

Author and bass angler Monte Burch, shown here at the controls of a Bass Cat "Cougar" boat, has witnessed the development of the modern bass boat. He has personally tested and rated many of the most popular models.

Chapter 2

Bass Boat Design and Construction

A pad or flat running surface at the stern portion of the hull sets bass boats, such as the Nitro shown above, apart from most other boat designs.

My first experience with bass fishing came long before the popularity of bass boats. An old wooden Johnboat provided the means to explore the backwater sloughs of the rivers near my home. Then along came aluminum John boats and I eventually graduated to them. I bought my first for-real fishing boat, a fiberglass Sears Gamefisher, rigged with a McCulloch motor and thought it didn't get any better. Then came a Terry bass boat, and a number of years after that I finally graduated into a full-blown bass boat. I've seen a lot of changes, and believe me, today's modern bass boats are a far cry from those of the "good ol' days." Built of modern materials and with design refinements and technology unavailable just a few years ago, today's bass boat represents the ultimate in comfort, safety and functional utility.

In times past bass anglers relegated themselves to small areas of larger rivers and lakes simply because they lacked engines of sufficient size to risk open water or to cover much distance. The modern bass boat -- hydrodynamically and aerodynamically designed for higher speed operation -- can carry larger capacity loads, bigger horsepower engines, and provides bass anglers with an operating range not imagined in the days when we fished within sight of the dock. Bass boats are becoming bigger and bigger, reaching sizes formerly relegated to some saltwater boats.

BASS BOAT DESIGN

Bass boats have several features that set them apart from most other types of boats. The first is hull design. Even relatively underpowered bass boats are designed for speed. While quite a bit of variance is found in the bow shape of today's bass boats, the sterns all have one thing in common: a running pad. This is basically the line where the "V" comes from the bow, and continues along the keel to the stern. On most other boat styles, including runabouts, deep-V lake boats, and most saltwater boats, the V-shape continues from the bow to the end of the transom. This keeps the boat from rolling from side to side in wakes and rollers.

Most bass boats feature relatively flat transoms. Exceptions are boats built by Charger and Ranger. Charger was the first to design a bass boat with a built-in setback. This design sets the engine back and features a series of vertical steps to position the engine farther from the bottom of the transom. This removes the engine from the disturbance created by the boat's displacement and into cleaner water. The results are better hole shots, greater top-end speeds, and better maneuverability. Ranger utilizes a solid fiberglass transom with a built-in setback to provide the same advantages.

Bass boats are primarily designed to be used as fishing platforms in relatively calm water. Therefore the "V" has been reduced and a flat pad

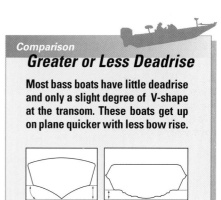

Comparison

Greater or Less Deadrise

Most bass boats have little deadrise and only a slight degree of V-shape at the transom. These boats get up on plane quicker with less bow rise.

Greater Deadrise   Less Deadrise

Bass boats with higher deadrise tend to wallow when getting up on plane. They also bank more on turns while those with a shallow deadrise turn flatter. In addition, craft with a greater deadrise roll more while at rest and are less stable than boats with less deadrise.

Deep-V vs. Slim Silhouette

Deep-V Forward
Some bass boats feature a fairly deep-V forward of the pad, which provides better handling in rough water.

Slimmer "Silhouette" Forward
Boats, such as this Allison design, feature slimmer "silhouette" forward hulls for more speed.

An important factor influencing the performance characteristics of the two main bass boat types is the amount of deep-V forward. A boat with deeper "V" tends to run slower due to the friction caused by greater water contact and wind resistance. Good examples of deeper "V" forward boats are the Charger and Champion models. Superfast boats have more of a streamlined, "stiletto" forward providing reduced wind and water resistance and less forward weight. Examples of these boats include models by Bullet, Gambler, and Allison.

There's another trade-off to be aware of. The deeper "V" bass boats tend to have a greater draft and can't handle shallow water as well as the flatter hull designs. On the other hand, boats with a deeper "V" forward handle much more easily in rough water and tend to track truer with trolling motors. Many bass boats fall between the two extremes, with a medium or modified forward "V" to maintain stability in waves and at slow speeds and then thinning back to a pad. The amount of bow flare varies as well. Some bows sweep outward to push water out and away. This produces a very dry ride even in rough water.

built into the hull just before the transom. This pad is the main design feature that sets bass boats apart. The hulls are designed so the bow rises out of the water and the boat runs on the pad. This gives bass boats their speed. The size and configuration of the running pad varies widely from manufacturer to manufacturer and is a major factor in how different bass boats perform at higher speeds.

"You can take a 65 mph boat and, with a little sanding and Bondo, turn it into a 70 mph boat," explained Mike Causey of Charger Boats. "In attempting to get even more performance out of a particular hull, I made at least two dozen trips to the lake for exploratory runs, after reworking the pad." This doesn't mean you can do the same thing with your boat. Mike was designing a prototype that would be used to make a mold for a new fiberglass hull.

Bass boats can be classed into two categories — although manufacturers and many drivers don't like the idea. There are what I call normal-but-fast bass boats. Then there are the "hot rod" bass boats, some of which are capable of reaching speeds of over 90 mph. While most boat drivers wouldn't admit it, the average bass-boater can't handle these top speeds. Once you get over the mile-per-minute mark, the design of the boat, location of the engine,

and driver's skills all become extremely important. A heck of a lot can happen in a fraction of a second!

SAFETY

Old-time boats offered few safety features. The hull designs were tippy and if the boat filled with water, it sank. Boats that rowed or paddled well often performed poorly when outboard power was added. Today's bass boats all feature positive flotation. Forrest Wood, president of Ranger Boat Company, pushed for the positive flotation feature for years before the Coast Guard made it a requirement. Ranger injects every non-storage space with an expanding polyurethane foam material. Applied to the gunwales and between the deck and hull, this thick substance rapidly expands to many times its original volume, filling most of the areas with a material that becomes a rigid part of the structure and provides the necessary flotation.

SIZE

The earliest bass boats were as short as 14 feet in length, but 16-footers quickly became the norm. I remember riding as an observer many years ago at a U.S. Bass Million Dollar Tournament when all contest-

Bass boats range from 16-footers up to boats that are 22 feet in length. The larger boats, such as this Skeeter, are extremely popular.

ants fished out of the same 16-foot boat. The tournament was held on Sam Rayburn Lake and, I swear, the distance between the 4-foot chops was exactly 15 feet. We got beat to death.

Bass boats have gradually increased in size and are now available in lengths of up to 22 feet; 18- and 19-foot models remain the most popular. The larger boats offer advantages and disadvantages. Their ride is softer and the bigger boats can carry more fuel, equipment, and tackle. They also accommodate more people, an important consideration for fishing guides. The main disadvantage is weight. Big boats require heavier and more powerful trolling motors which tend to make them sit lower in the water. With a deeper draft they are at greater risk from underwater obstacles.

FIBERGLASS

Fiberglass is the most common bass boat material. Fiberglass construction utilizes various types of glass filaments -- loose matt, woven, and strand – which are mixed with various thermo-setting resins to create a laminated hull or deck. More high-tech

materials may be added to the laminate, including Kevlar and carbon fiber. The well-proven process is called fiberglass reinforced plastic (FRP). Fiberglass can be molded into just about any shape you can think of. FRP construction requires a female mold in which the boat is formed. Gelcoats, which form the outside of the boat, are placed in the mold and the laminates are added. This creates an extremely shiny and maintenance-free finish with a wide range of color and exterior patterns. Fiberglass also has a "memory." If struck by an obstacle, unless the lamination is broken, it springs back to the original shape. Fiberglass does, however, tend to chalk and fade over time.

While some manufacturers use composite materials for stringers, floors, and structural elements, fiberglass boats have been traditionally constructed with wooden interior components. In days past, when bass boat construction was in its infancy, boats with wooden interiors got a bad name due to the problems with rot. Many high-quality bass boats are still constructed with wooden structural members but modern boatbuilders understand

the danger of allowing water to get into the interior structure during construction. Specially treated woods, designed just for the marine industry, resist rot, fungus, and weathering.

Comparison
Chines – Round vs. Hard

The design of the chines on a bass boat hull influences both its handling and maneuverability.

| Round Chine | Hard Chine |

Boats have either round, "soft," square, or "hard" chines. Most bass boat hulls feature hard chines, which create a definite joint at the hull bottom and sides. Round chines provide the softest ride but offer less stability. A square chine provides easy planing, good water deflection, greater stability, and requires less horsepower to run the boat at higher speeds. The number and shape of planing strakes also has an effect. They provide lift to get the hull on plane. Several larger and flatter strakes create a boat with a firmer ride and better control on turns.

Charger Fiberglass Boat Construction

I've toured a number of boat-manufacturing plants, and fiberglass bass boats are actually made somewhat different than many people imagine. The following steps from Charger illustrate the basic fiberglass boat construction.

1. THE MOLD

"The thing many people don't understand about fiberglass bass boats is, you build them from the outside in," said Mike Causey from Charger.

Fiberglass Construction
- Fiberglass is the most popular bass boat material.
- Fiberglass bass boats are built using special forms or molds taken directly from the designer's prototype.
- Fiberglass boats are built from the outside in.

Gelcoat and Paint
- The first step is to apply a clear gelcoat to the female portion of the mold. This forms the outside protective coating for the boat.
- Any pin stripe or other design is masked off on the inside of the gelcoat using tape or other masking material.
- With all of the stripe designs masked off, polliflake and more gelcoat are sprayed into the mold, creating a prism of vibrant colors on the exterior surface.
- Several layers of paint are applied, producing a rich, deep, and lustrous finish.
- The masking material is removed to expose the trademark stripe designs.
- The detail and stripe colors are sprayed into the areas left by removing the mask.
- The bass boat hull now has its final outside finish.

2. LAMINATION

"The woven roving is what provides the strength," said Causey, "and makes a boat really tough."

Building Up the Body
- At Charger the lamination process begins with the application of a skin of chopped strand matt.
- The chopped strand matt is wetted out with resin and worked down with a hand roller to make sure that there are no air pockets and that the glass and resin are well mixed together.

Application of the Woven Roving
- Once the first layer of matt is down, the hull is built up with layers of chopped and woven fiberglass strands or "woven roving."
- The transom is clamped in while the glass is wet and solidly locked in place.
- A special coating is applied around all edges of the transom to make sure the fiberglass has no voids in it.
- Several layers of woven roving are applied tying the transom to the sides and bottom of the hull.

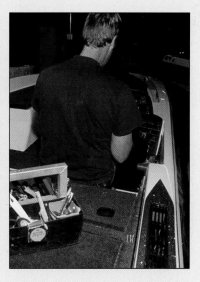

3. BUILDING THE HULL

Constructing the Stringers

- The stringers, the bass boat's backbone system, are placed in the bottom of the boat.
- Charger uses top-quality, pressure-treated marine plywood for its stringers, floor, and boxes.
- More woven roving is added to bind the stringers to the hull.
- The stringers are fiberglassed in.
- The floor components are installed and everything is glassed down.

Injecting Foam

- Foam is forced into all the voids under the floor and into the foam boxes through holes drilled in their tops.
- Once the foam spaces are filled, the holes are sealed and the foam is allowed to dry.

Lifting the Boat from the Mold

- Before applying the initial paint and gelcoat, the inside of the mold is coated with wax so that the hull will separate from the mold.
- The boat is attached to a chain hoist, air is injected between the hull and the mold, and the hull is lifted out.

4. DETAILS & DECK

Completing the Hull

- The boat moves to the hull-completion station and the gunwales are prepared so that the railing can be attached with screws.
- Charger uses solid oak wood for this attachment area.
- All through-the-hull fittings in the rear of the boat are installed.
- Carpeting is laid and glued in place in the interior spaces.

Deck Construction

- The deck is constructed in the same basic manner as the hull. It's painted first, all the fiberglass work is completed, and the reinforcements and various boxes are installed.
- Once the deck has cured, it's lifted from the mold.
- While it's still upside down, carpeting is fitted and all the wiring and plumbing are installed.
- The deck is flipped over and holes are cut for the instrument panel.
- The gauges, instrument panel, and controls are installed.
- All rails and cleats are fitted.

5. JOINING DECK & HULL

Fitting the Deck

- The deck is flipped over, shiny side up.
- The deck and hull are joined together using a shoebox fit. The deck is screwed down and coated with fiberglass and the joint is concealed with a gunwale rail.
- Once the final detail work is complete the entire boat is cleaned and the deck and hull are polished and waxed.

Final Interior Work

- Carpet is applied to the inside of the boxes, the storage boxes are trimmed out, and all the hardware is attached.
- All compartment lids are then installed on the top of the deck.
- The seats are upholstered and installed.
- Once the final detail work is complete the entire boat is cleaned and the deck and hull are polished and waxed.
- If the boat is to be rigged at the plant, the engine is mounted and the trolling motor installed.
- The unit is then set on a trailer, and it's ready to go.

For years, fiberglass has been the most common bass boat building material, as shown on this Stratos. Fiberglass can be molded into almost any shape you can image and it has "memory".

Wooden structural members are bonded into the hull with better resins and adhesives to create stronger, longer-lasting, joints.

WOOD FREE

Composite structural components definitely do not rot, and tend to be lighter than similar wooden parts. Composite structural elements, sometimes strengthened with foam, create a monohull design. Manufacturers Ranger and Triton offer wood-free construction. Triton boats are built with a unibody construction that offers superior strength while reducing performance-robbing weight. Triton's stringer system uses Tri-Core, a strong super-polyurethane core material. According to Triton, structural tests show Tri-Core to be approximately 1/3 lighter than wood, yet two times stronger than wood/fiberglass laminate.

Triton's one-piece fiberglass Zero-Flex stringer system features two braces running from bow to stern with cross-members connecting port to starboard. This design makes Triton boats extremely rigid and helps prevent the deck and hull from twisting. The composite transom is bonded to the stringer system with hi-density com-

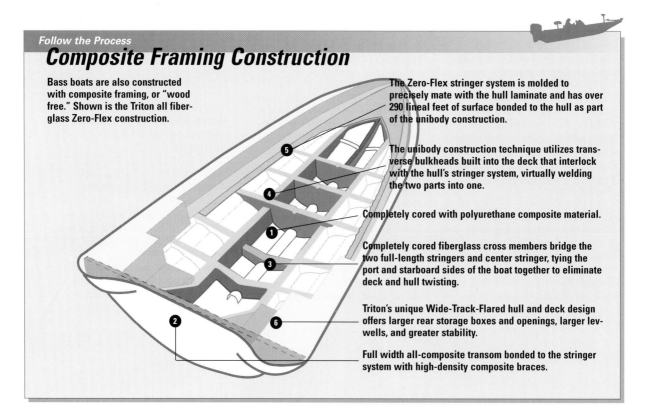

Follow the Process
Composite Framing Construction

Bass boats are also constructed with composite framing, or "wood free." Shown is the Triton all fiberglass Zero-Flex construction.

The Zero-Flex stringer system is molded to precisely mate with the hull laminate and has over 290 lineal feet of surface bonded to the hull as part of the unibody construction.

The unibody construction technique utilizes transverse bulkheads built into the deck that interlock with the hull's stringer system, virtually welding the two parts into one.

Completely cored with polyurethane composite material.

Completely cored fiberglass cross members bridge the two full-length stringers and center stringer, tying the port and starboard sides of the boat together to eliminate deck and hull twisting.

Triton's unique Wide-Track-Flared hull and deck design offers larger rear storage boxes and openings, larger lev-wells, and greater stability.

Full width all-composite transom bonded to the stringer system with high-density composite braces.

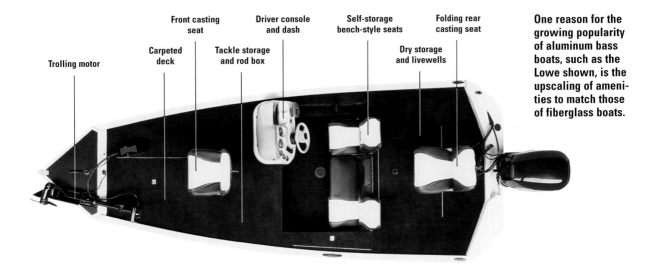

Trolling motor · Carpeted deck · Front casting seat · Tackle storage and rod box · Driver console and dash · Self-storage bench-style seats · Dry storage and livewells · Folding rear casting seat

One reason for the growing popularity of aluminum bass boats, such as the Lowe shown, is the upscaling of amenities to match those of fiberglass boats.

posite braces. The unibody construction technique utilizes transverse bulkheads built into the deck interlock with the hull's stringer system, virtually welding the two parts into one. The Zero-Flex stringer system is molded to precisely mate with the hull laminate.

A type of fiberglass/composite construction, called Virtually Engineered Composites (VEC), was pioneered by Genmar and is used in their Ranger boats. Two forms are used in this closed, pressure molding process. Gelcoat is applied inside the female mold and a fiber material called Bitex is cut to match the various hull shapes and placed in the mold. At the same time, urethane foam sections, precisely molded to form the floor, stringer system, and storage boxes are placed in the mold. The male mold is lowered into position, and catalyzed resin is pumped into the cavities to thoroughly saturate the fiberglass. The entire system is held in water at a temperature of 124 degrees F. The hull cures in a little over a half hour. When the hull comes out of the mold it has the composite structural system, including the floor, and all backing plates for

the engine and hardware, solidly secured in place.

Full composite boats, especially those with foam or balsa cores, are much lighter and stronger and require less reinforcement. Composite hulls are found in the high-end, high-performance boats, such as Bullet and Allison. Stratos has been experimenting with a total Kevlar, carbon-fiber boat.

ALUMINUM

Many first-time buyers are faced with the choice of fiberglass or aluminum. For value and durability, aluminum is hard to beat. A good aluminum boat can cost considerably less than a comparable fiberglass model. A buyer should avoid boats that use wood in the transom or other areas. Wood will eventually rot and cause costly repairs.

Aluminum bass boats tend to ride higher in the water making them better for stump- and snag-filled waters. On the other hand, they're noisier and a bit harder to control in the wind. In addition

aluminum is a soft metal. As Mike Causey points out: "You put a dent in aluminum and it's there. It doesn't have memory like fiberglass." Aluminum, however, is easier to repair than fiberglass. It can be re-welded, patched, and minor dents can be pounded back in shape.

Several aluminum boat makers have switched to welded construction which reduces leakage from loosened rivets. Welded bass boats offer less water resistance and have fewer maintenance problems. In the past aluminum bass boats had a boxy appearance because traditional construction consisted of assembling flat pieces of aluminum into a boxy shape. Some manufacturers are now using improved metal forming techniques to create more aesthetically pleasing, better performing aluminum bass boats. Xpress was the first with their Hyper-Lift Hull. It uses a number of "breaks," or bends, to create the chines and strakes of the hull. The remainder of the boat is welded. Modern aluminum, all-welded hulls have the performance characteristics of fiberglass boats.

Chapter 3

Outboards

Outboard engines for bass boats can range in size from a modest 40 horsepower up to massive 300 horsepower models. The most popular motors are in the 150 range.

Most bass boats are outboard powered with motors available in a wide selection of horsepower ranging from two all the way up to 300. Selecting the proper outboard for your bass boat is as important as selecting the boat that best suits your style of fishing. Buyers will find that manufacturers frequently offer package deals with specific brands and sizes of outboards selected for their boats. In many instances, these engines have been tested on the manufacturer's boat models to determine the best performance. Several models of one brand may be available, however, and a buyer would do well to consult the performance charts for the engine and boat combination that they are interested in. Outboards are generally sold through dealers along with the boats. It can be important to rely on your dealer to help mate the correct motor and boat.

SIZE

When I first started with bass boats a 50 horsepower motor got you there fast enough. By the time bass tournament fishing had come into full swing, the average size motor had blossomed to 150 horsepower. Motors stayed at that size for several years under the horsepower restriction placed by B.A.S.S. on participants in their tournaments. These days 200s are quite common, with many bass anglers running 225s, 250s, and even 300s, on their boats.

It's important to match the size of the motor to your boat. Remember – a boat's highest rated engine may not necessarily provide the best handling and performance characteristics. Many factors, including the weight of the engine, can affect the handling in some boats.

Unfortunately not every manufacturer measures torque the same way. Some measure at the crankshaft and others at the prop shaft. Crank- shafts have a lot of torque, but some of that power is lost as it makes its way down through a multitude of gears to the propeller. As a result, an engine measured at the crankshaft will get a higher horsepower rating than one measured at the prop shaft. Since it is the propeller that actually moves the boat, engines measured at the prop shaft get horsepower ratings that more realistically reflect their power.

An engine's gear ratio can dramatically affect its ability to accelerate, propel heavy loads, and move at top-end speeds. Propeller design affects power as well. Other factors affecting power include boat weight, drive-train efficiency, engine reliability, maintenance, driving style, and even weather. Bass boaters should look beyond horsepower rating to get an engine that is properly matched to their needs.

The first step in determining the horsepower you want is to check the boat for a Coast Guard rated maximum horsepower certificate. Rating tags are required on all outboard hulls under 20 feet and will be attached to the interior. This maximum horsepower figure does not mean that it is the most ideal horsepower for the boat, but rather indicates the top limit of power for safe operation. Most bass boat hulls will perform quite well without using the absolute top limit of power. It is extremely important, however, not to exceed the maximum rated horsepower limit of any hull. Appropriately powering your boat is the first rule of boating safety.

FEATURES

One important feature to look for in a motor is loop-charged fuel induction, rather than cross-charged. A loop-charged engine delivers greater power and economy. Spent gases are forced out of the cylinder while any unburned fuel is forced back through and burned up. Yamaha has a patented sensor that measures the oxygen content of the exhaust gases to calculate how much oxygen is present. The engine automatically adjusts the amount of fuel to each cylinder to maximize power and fuel economy.

If purchasing a two-stroke engine, select one with oil injection (most larger bass boat engines now have this feature). Oil injection eliminates the need to mix oil and gas. Your motor will run

better and last longer. Look for an oil-injection system that injects oil directly into the manifold for better performance. Two-stroke outboards mix oil with gas for lubrication. Older motors typically use twice the oil of newer motors. Less oil means less blue smoke and a longer life. Be sure to use only Boating Industry Association (BIA) certified two-cycle oil in your outboard.

Engine protection varies quite a bit, but quality engine manufacturers build in sensors to help prevent damage from over-revving, overheating, and low engine oil. The systems typically use buzzers, horns, lights, and some automatically decrease the rpm of the engine gradually, to protect against further damage. Corrosion protection is another important feature. Sacrificial zinc anodes are designed to attract corrosive elements, protecting the engine. Modern fishing accessories like livewells, fish finders, and radios need power. A high-output charging system

Outboard Motor Profiles

HONDA

- Honda is the undisputed leader in four-stroke outboards, having produced them for more than 35 years.

- Their outboards have proven to be so reliable that the company backs them with a warranty that includes three years of non-declining coverage. This is the longest, most complete warranty offered by any outboard manufacturer.

- Honda also offers an extensive lineup of outboard engines, ranging from their tiny two-horsepower to their mid-range 115- and 130-horsepower engines. The latter two were introduced in 1997 and at that time were the most powerful four-strokes on the market.

- Honda now has a V-6 four-stroke outboard that can produce up to 225 horsepower. It is ideal for the higher-horsepower freshwater applications.

- The Honda models are available in both 200- and 225-horsepower versions, and meet EPA emission regulations for the year 2006 and the more stringent California Air Resources Board (CARB) emissions standards for 2008.

- The engines feature programmed electronic fuel injection, an engine command module that manages engine function, an engine alert system and a SOHC, four-valves-per-cylinder, 3471cc engine that is compact and powerful. One of the main features is an On-Demand 60-amp, automobile-proven, belt-driven alternator.

YAMAHA

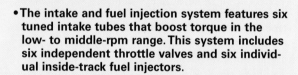

- Yamaha beat Honda to the game by introducing their F225 and F200 in the summer of 2001.

- These engines feature a unique 3.3-liter 60-degree V6 DOHC power unit designed to deliver high-combustion efficiency and high-power output.

- They feature Yamaha's Double Overhead Cam technology that includes 24 valves for precise valve timing and better fuel economy.

- The intake and fuel injection system features six tuned intake tubes that boost torque in the low- to middle-rpm range. This system includes six independent throttle valves and six individual inside-track fuel injectors.

- These outboards feature a unique idle-speed controller and idle noise-reduction system that ensures quiet operation throughout the entire rpm range.

- One of the best features, however, is the weight and size. The F225 at 583 pounds is almost the same size as a two-stroke outboard of the same class. And it's only 52 pounds heavier than a competitor's 225-horsepower two-stroke V6.

- Yamaha also has several other four-strokes, including their 1.0 liter in-line four-cylinder engine block, the F60. It is engineered for smaller-sized boats to provide economical and quiet power.

- A high-thrust four-stroke T8, eight horsepower, combines low gear ratios with dual-thrust propeller, for 70 percent more thrust and 60 percent more reverse thrust and superior braking.

SUZUKI

- Suzuki jumped ahead in the mid-range motors for bass boats with their DF140, a four-cylinder, in-line, electronic fuel-injected outboard that is extremely compact yet powerful enough to provide excellent performance on the larger aluminum and mid-sized fiberglass bass boats.

- The engine weighs less than any comparable fuel-injected four-stroke or direct-injected two-stroke presently in production.

- The DF140 is based on Suzuki's in-line four-cylinder powerhead with offset drive shaft for compact size and a rigged-and-ready weight of only 410 pounds (20-inch shaft model). An exclusive engine cover design with a large air induction port provides maximum airflow for increased power.

- Suzuki features a compact in-line, four-block with dual overhead cams and four valves per cylinder. Cylinders are bored to 86mm for total displacement of 2044cc. A two-stage cam drive allows for a smaller cylinder head and reduced valve angles.

- Power is delivered from the crankshaft via a primary reduction gear and offset driveshaft located under the powerhead. Besides lowering the height of the powerhead, this system moves the engine's center of gravity forward and contributes to better balance over the transom. The second-stage gear reduction in the gear case provides a 2.38:1 gear ratio that allows the DF140 to turn a larger prop (both in diameter and pitch).

- The DF140 features Suzuki's multipoint sequential electronic fuel injection, matched to the long-track intake manifold and 4-into-2-into-1 exhaust system. The DF140 is also the first four-stroke outboard to feature a bolt-on, water-cooled oil cooler. The 2044cc engine delivers the greatest power-to-displacement ratio in the four-stroke market.

MERCURY

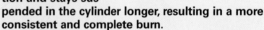

- Mercury continues to place their money on big horsepower motors and on their proven OptiMax two-strokes.

- Mercury engines use a two-stage DFI process. A burst of air (at 80 psi) shoots through the fuel, breaking it into a fine mist. This fine mist creates more surface area for combustion and stays suspended in the cylinder longer, resulting in a more consistent and complete burn.

- The OptiMax is the first two-stroke with direct fuel injection to meet EPA certification for 2006 and CARB.

- Mercury has a lineup of four-strokes in the smaller horsepower range. The BigFoot family of engines includes 9.9, 15, 25, 40, 50, and 60. Designed for larger-displacement hulls, they incorporate stronger, more durable gears and can utilize larger propellers.

- Mercury also holds a place the lower end of the mid-range market with their 30, 40, 50, 60, 75, 90, and 115-EFI Four Stroke motors. The 115EFI is the first advanced electronic fuel injection four-stroke offered by Mercury and features a microcomputer-controlled CDL ignition. The 115EFI has in-line four-cylinders with dual overhead cams for smooth running operation. For their onboard electronics, Mercury has incorporated a 25-amp alternator system. Both the 50 and 60 are the first "all-Mercury" engines, featuring super-quiet operation, maintenance-free design and 15-amp charging.

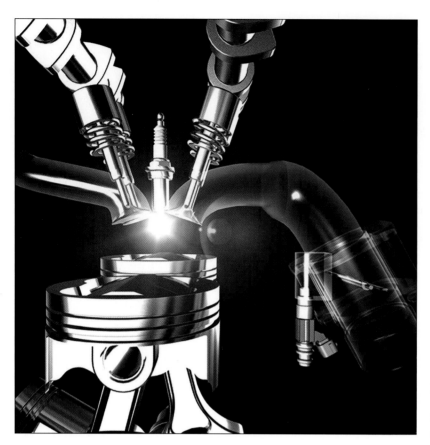

Two-stroke technology has come a long way, with most quality two-stroke engines now featuring some sort of electronic fuel injection. Yamaha features their High Pressure Direct Injection.

TWO-STROKE TECHNOLOGY

Conventional two-stroke carbureted engines deliver the fuel/oil charge up from the bottom of the piston. The exhaust port is partially open as the piston moves the fuel/oil charge up. The mixture then passes up and around the piston to reach the top of the cylinder head for combustion. Some of the mixture escapes through the partially open exhaust port. Since the spark plug can only fire after the piston completely covers the exhaust port, some fuel efficiency is lost.

Fuel injection has pretty well replaced the old carbureted fuel systems on outboards. The first fuel injection systems were mechanical, followed by electronic fuel injection (EFI). The timing

produces plenty of power to keep batteries charged, even while idling. Look for a system with at least 25-amp output.

TWO-STROKE OR FOUR-STROKE

For years, two-stroke outboards were the norm for bass boats. This was primarily due to the size of engine required. Within recent years manufacturers, including Honda, Suzuki, and Yamaha, have developed four-strokes with more than enough power to drive the biggest bass boats. Mercury and Johnson/Evinrude continue to bet their money on the higher-horsepower two-stroke motors with direct fuel injection (DFI) high-tech clean-fuel systems. All engines must meet the Environmental Protection Agency regulations set for 2006. The California Air Resources Board, however, has set an even more stringent regulation. You will not be able to purchase new-model two-stroke motors in California after 2008.

OMC Ficht Ram Injection blasts short bursts of fuel directly into the combustion chamber.

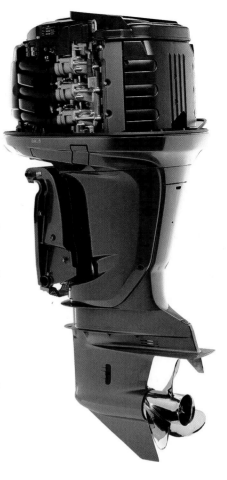

Four-stroke engines offer several advantages, including lower noise levels, eliminating the hassle of combining oil and gas, and emit fewer emissions to both water and land.

and amount of fuel injected is controlled by various electric signals sent from an electronic engine controller (EEC). The computer controller monitors engine-operating conditions such as coolant, air, oil temperature, engine speed and load, velocity, and throttle position. This information is processed by programs in the computer to provide optimum fuel delivery and timing control which results in more powerful, smoother-running engines with better fuel economy and greatly reduced emissions.

EFI is available in different forms. The first was throttle-body injection of the type used in automobiles. The next step was multi-port fuel injection that provided even greater efficiency. Ultimately direct fuel injection (DFI) produced the cleanest, most powerful two-strokes available for bass boats. Direct fuel injection brings the oil in from the bottom of the piston while the fuel is delivered via a fuel rail and injectors from the top of the piston. The engine is designed to wait until the exhaust port is closed before the fuel is directed down into the cylinder head. A precise amount of fuel can be delivered at exactly the right time. The process allows for a more complete burn that substantially reduces emissions.

The various manufacturers all came about DFI in different ways. Yamaha engineers developed the High Pressure Direct Injection system pressurizing the fuel to 700 psi, making an improved atomiza-tion for a more complete burn.

The OMC Ficht Ram Injection system uses electromagnetic solenoid-driven fuel injector pumps, controlled by a powerful microprocessor-based engine management system, to blast short bursts of fuel directly into the combustion chamber at rates of up to 100 times-per-second, at pressures up to 450 psi. This improves throttle response and overall performance throughout the mid-ranges of the power band. Since the Ficht Ram injection system is designed to inject raw fuel directly into the cylinder, the powerhead includes a separate oiling system, which injects the precise amount of lubricating oil into the engine at lubrication points.

FOUR-STROKE TECHNOLOGY

I did it twice – tried to start a Suzuki 140-horsepower four-stroke while it was already running. Granted, I'm hard of hearing, but several other boating writers did the same thing during the introduction of the motor in Key Largo, Florida. That's one of the major advantages four-strokes offer bass anglers: they don't roar, they purr like a big cat.

Lower operating-noise isn't the only advantage four-strokes offer. Without the addition of oil to the fuel there are fewer emissions into the air and water and generally fuel costs are lower than with two-strokes. Honda tests show

that boats operated with four-stroke engines have 50-percent greater range at top speed and 200-percent greater range at trolling speed than boats with two-stroke motors on the same amount of fuel.

Many of the older upper-range horsepower four-stroke motors were quite heavy. I once tested a 130 horsepower on a 16-foot fiberglass bass boat, and while the motor performed well, the boat produced a tremendous amount of backwash after shut down. At rest the boat actually sat with the rear of the transom almost under water. Outboard manufacturers have worked hard to reduce the weight and the bulkiness of the

Engine Operation Checklist

While modern outboard engines are designed to tolerate a lot of abuse, regular maintenance is a key to a long-lived motor. Many maintenance procedures and repairs should not be attempted at home because of safety problems, the possibility of voiding your warranty, or even the chance of ruining your motor. There are other chores, however, that you can easily do for yourself. Your motor should be winterized each fall and then serviced before each boating season. Ideally, your motor should be taken to an authorized dealer at least once a year for lubricant change, water pump check, tune-up, and so forth.

BEFORE EACH USE:

1. Check to make sure the lanyard stop switch stops the engine.

2. Inspect the fuel system for deterioration or leaks.

3. Check outboard for tightness on transom.

4. Check steering system for binding or loose components.

5. Check steering link rod fasteners for proper tightness.

AFTER EACH USE:

1. Flush out the outboard cooling system if the bass boat has been operating in salt or polluted water.

2. If operating in salt water, wash off salt deposits and flush the propeller and gear case exhaust outlet with fresh water.

3. Check the propeller blades for possible damage.

YEARLY OR AFTER 100 HOURS OF USE
(whichever occurs first):

1. Lubricate all lubrication points. Lubricate more frequently when used in salt water. Examine the motor for oil seepage or oil marks on the ground. If you find any leaks, you should take the engine to your dealer to have new seals installed.

2. Grease the throttle cable, steering handle bracket, and all other moving parts, pivot points, or grease zerks. Ask your dealer for a non-fibrous marine grease that adheres tightly and won't melt in the heat, break down in salt water, or become sticky and stiff. Spray the entire engine with a light lubricant. The spray protects rubber, plastic, paint, and metal from corrosion caused by salt and other elements. It also reduces sticking in moving parts.

3. Give your motor a "shock treatment" by mixing a fuel additive with the gasoline during the first hours of springtime operation. A good fuel additive cleans away harmful deposits caused by unleaded fuel. It safely cleans carbon and varnish from rings, pistons, ports, valves, intake and exhaust manifolds, jets, carburetors and combustion chambers in two- and four-cycle engines.

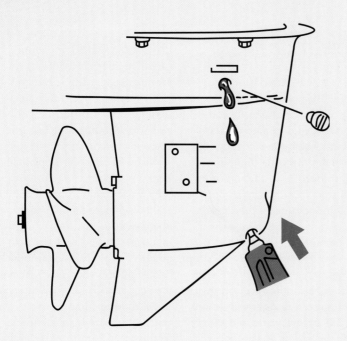

4. Inspect and clean spark plugs. Remove the spark plug leads and inspect the spark plug boots and leads, and replace if cracked. Remove the spark plugs and inspect and/or clean. Replace the spark plug if it is worn or the insulator is rough, cracked, broken, blistered or fouled. Clean away dirt on the spark plug seats and install plugs finger tight, then tighten 1/4 turn or torque to the specs in the owner's manual.

5. Check the fuel system. Inspect the fuel line and primer bulb for cracks, leaks, hardening, or other signs of deterioration. Replace if necessary. On carbureted engines check the fuel line filter for contaminants. If the line appears to be contaminated, remove and replace. It is also important to inspect the filter connections for leaks by squeezing the primer bulb until firm to force fuel through the filter. On EFI models inspect the water-separating filter. Dry if necessary. Replace the filter if it is plugged with debris.

6. Check corrosion-control anodes – the gray, unpainted pieces of zinc attached to the lower unit. The anodes protect your motor from galvanic corrosion. Check anodes regularly if your boat is in salt water, especially if it is moored for long periods of time. The anodes will erode and should be replaced before they become completely degraded. Never paint or apply a protective coating to the anode, as this will reduce its effectiveness.

7. Drain and replace gear-case lubricant. Remove the fill plug and washer. Always use the lubricant prescribed by the engine manufacturer. Remove vent screw and washer. Never add lubricant to the gear housing without first removing the vent screw. Add lubricant until the excess begins to flow out of the vent hole. Next drain off about an ounce of lubricant to permit expansion. Replace the vent screw and fill plug along with their washers.

8. Check power-trim fluid. Add the appropriate fluid as needed.

9. Inspect battery.

10. Remove engine deposits with the appropriate engine cleaner.

11. Check tightness of bolts, nuts and other fasteners.

Proper Motor Mounts

There are two important steps that must be taken to assure a proper motor mount. First, position the motor squarely in the center of the transom on the center line (keel line) to assure that the boat is well balanced. If the motor is off center, the boat will be hard to steer. If your boat has an asymmetrical keel, consult your dealer.

The motor should be mounted at the proper height to provide optimum efficiency with the least amount of water resistance, or drag. The mounting height of the outboard greatly affects water resistance. If a motor is mounted too low, it will cause excessive drag, resulting in poor handling and high fuel consumption. If mounted too high, cavitation will cause poor handling and reduced propulsion. In cases where the propeller tips cut air, the engine rpm can rise abnormally causing the motor to overheat. Most manufacturers suggest mounting the motor so the anti-cavitation plate is between the bottom of the boat and a level line 1 inch below it.

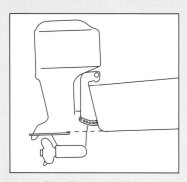

Center Mounting the Motor

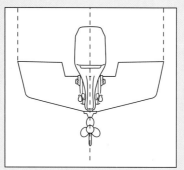

Proper Mounting Height

earlier motors.

At one time, many fishermen thought that four-strokes could not possibly reach 100 horsepower. These days, however, four-strokes are available in all the horsepower ranges, from tiny 5s to the big 225s. The latter will push even the big 20-foot bass boats with ease. A current bass boat trend of the past few years is the appearance of a number of high-performance, pad-style, aluminum boats. More economical to purchase, tow, and run, these boats are becoming increasingly popular. I've tested a number of these boats with 90- and 115-horsepower motors, and all have performed extremely well. Certain ranges – what I call the mid-range engines for bass boats – such as the Honda 130 and Suzuki 140, all perform extremely well on the larger aluminum and smaller fiberglass boats.

ENGINE INSTALLATION

Installing larger engines requires special tools – including a heavy-duty hoist – particular attention to mounting, and not a little work. If you're handy with your hands, have a few tools and a garage to work in (or perhaps a handy shade tree), the job is possible. Installing smaller models, or those up to 30 horsepower without extra features, is a fairly simple hang-on job. Models 40 horsepower and up, those with power tilt or electric start, require a bit more effort, depending on the motor and boat combination.

Mounting an outboard motor requires attention to detail. Even a small outboard improperly mounted can create hazardous boating conditions. The first step is to make sure you don't overpower the boat with a bigger horsepower motor than the maximum power rating. Check the capacity plate – if the boat doesn't have a capacity rating, consult the boat manufacturer. Since motors come either long or short shaft, the transom height of your boat will determine the shaft length you'll need. You can install a long-shaft motor on a standard-height transom by using a transom elevator (made by T & R Marine) – an aluminum block that fits down over the transom and raises the engine 5 inches.

The best mounting height for the outboard is determined by the boat and motor combination and the planned use. By testing at different heights, you can determine the optimum position. During a water test with the boat at rest, check the buoyancy of the boat while empty and with a full load. Make sure the static water level on the exhaust housing is low enough to prevent water entry into the powerhead due to waves when the outboard is not running. Always check for design peculiarities, obstructions, and accessories that might prevent a smooth flow of water. Engines can be damaged by excessive water spray. For more precise handling and fuel efficiency, a jackplate can be installed. When installing the motor do not use bolts, nuts or washers other than those packaged with the motor. After tightening in place, test run the motor and check again for tightness.

Tools needed for installation include a portable electric drill and drill bit to fit mounting bolts, and an appropriate set of wrenches for tightening the mounting bolts. A ruler and carpenter's square will help determine the keel center. In some cases, you may need to run a string line from the bow along the keel to find the exact centerline. A small ball peen hammer and set of screwdrivers complete the tool list. Clear marine sealant is required to seal off the bolts, and black plastic electrician's tape to cover electrical connections.

INSTALLATION STEPS

Determine the centerline of the boat and mark the location on the transom, then determine the centerline of the motor and make a matching mark. If the motor needs to be raised you can add a transom elevator. I made a transom elevator from a piece of pressure-treated 2 x 4 by cutting it to the height needed and rounding the corners for better appearance. Then I fastened it with 3-inch anchor bolts down through the top into the transom. This limits you to a 1½-inch height increase.

The motor is then lowered onto the transom, positioned precisely, and the bolt holes are marked. In some instances, you may be able to bore the boltholes using the engine-mounting holes as a guide. In other cases, you may have to remove the motor, bore the holes and reposition the motor. When using the latter method use a punch to precisely locate the boltholes. Always use a bit that matches the bolts and do not allow the drill bit to slide sideways producing off center holes. IT IS VERY IMPORTANT TO MAKE SURE THE BOLT-HOLES ARE PRECISELY POSITIONED AND DRILLED. Seat the motor, squeeze a bit of clear marine sealant such as StarBrite Silicone Sealant in each of the mounting holes, and tighten the bolts. This will force sealant out around the bolts. Use a soft cloth to wipe away excess sealant before it sets up.

If you are installing an electric-start motor, mount the battery and anchor it in place with a battery tray such as the rod-hold-down model from T-H Marine. When you attach the leads to the battery make sure the red lead is attached to the positive side.

Motors are either tiller, console, or stick steer. For console or stick steer, the controls are first mounted in the appropriate location. Before permanent installation, check the throttle, shift, and steering cables to make sure they work freely. Finally, connect the throttle, shift lever, and steering wheel or stick. You will have to run any wiring from the motor and install and attach the various gauges, such as tachometer and speedometer. On small boats with stick or tiller steering, you'll probably need to build and install a small console for controls such as the tach, tilt, bilge pump, and livewell switches.

PROPS

The propeller converts horsepower into forward motion, making it the most important element in the chain linking the engine's power to the water. The right propeller is determined by several factors, including hull design, weight of the boat, engine horsepower, and the engine mounting position. With some basic knowledge and a little help from a marine dealer, you can often improve acceleration, top-end speed, and fuel economy, simply by changing props.

In most instances, bass boat engines come with the manufacturer's "standard" propeller. In the case

Matching the correct prop to the boat hull and the engine is one of the most important factors in attaining the best performance and handling

Cavitation occurs when water flow cannot follow the contour of a fast-moving underwater object, such as the gear housing or propeller on an outboard motor. Cavitation causes the propeller to speed up, but the boat's speed is reduced. Common causes of cavitation are: (1) a bent propeller blade or damaged gear housing skeg; (2) raised burrs or sharp edges on the propeller or gear housing; (3) weeds or other debris snagged on the propeller or gear housing.

Ventilation, on the other hand, occurs when surface air or exhaust gases are introduced around the propeller, resulting in a speed-up of the propeller and reduced speed for the boat. Excessive ventilation is annoying and is usually caused by: (1) installing the motor too high on the transom; (2) motor is tilted out too far; (3) propeller diffuser ring is missing; (4) damaged prop or gear housing, which allows exhaust gases to escape between the propeller and gear housing.

Pitch

Pitch is defined as the theoretical distance a prop will travel through a solid medium during one revolution. A prop with 19-inch pitch would therefore travel 19 inches per revolution. Water isn't a solid medium, however, and a certain amount of slippage must be figured into this distance. Since pitch is more responsible for rpm on an inch-by-inch basis than diameter, bass boaters have more flexibility in altering pitch to improve their

of package boats, the motor is often fitted with a prop that is matched to the boat and motor; however, the prop is usually an economical version. For those who want more performance from their bass boat without changing the motor, a change of propeller may provide the needed edge.

PROP PERFORMANCE FACTORS

Diameter

One of the prop's constant dimensions is its diameter, which is the distance from the hub center to a blade tip, doubled. The boat and motor application and setup usually limits how much the diameter can be altered. Different engines accept different diameters, and they are not all interchangeable.

There is, however, some leeway for adjusting a prop's performance with diameter changes.

Generally it's beneficial to use the largest diameter prop possible. A large column of water displaced by the prop will generate more thrust than a small one, and can reduce the slip factor. Increasing the diameter will improve hole shot, especially on a heavy boat, and will also reduce cavitation. Going to extremes, however, can adversely affect performance. If the prop diameter is too large, it can reduce the engine's maximum rated rpm; if too small, it can create a cavitation situation and over-rev the engine.

The terms "cavitation" and "ventilation" are frequently used interchangeably by bass boat owners, but the phenomena are different and have different causes.

Props have different pitches -- the theoretical distance a prop will travel through a solid medium during one revolution. Changing to a prop with a different pitch can greatly alter the performance of a bass boat.

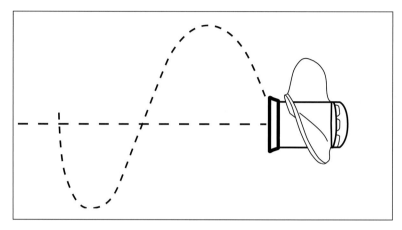

boat's performance. Most props are available in a variety of pitches, ranging from 16 to 28 degrees.

Pitch is analogous to gears on an automobile. A low-pitch angle will provide more power to accelerate and carry heavy loads, but reduces top speed. Conversely, a high-pitch prop will improve top-end speed, but reduce acceleration and the ability to shift heavy loads. That means boaters who want to obtain a quicker hole shot might choose a lower-pitch prop while those concerned with reaching the highest top-end speed may select a high-pitch prop. For bass boaters it is a trade-off -- we want good hole shots and high top-end speed.

The first step is to establish how your outboard and boat performs. Find the recommended rpm range for your engine at wide-open throttle (WOT) by referring to your engine owner's manual or conferring with your dealer. Outboards generally have WOT ranges of approximately 5,000 to 6,000 rpm. The next step

involves a simple dynamic test of your boat, motor, and propeller.

Find the maximum operational rpm for your boat and motor combination by running it at WOT. Before starting out, check the propeller to make sure it is not nicked, dinged, or bent. Run the boat with its normal load and weight distribution, and adjust the motor trim angle as necessary. Make a note of the maximum operation rpm at WOT. Compare to see if the engine is running in the manufacturer's recommended maximum-operation rpm range and determine the difference between the two. Deficiencies can sometimes be corrected by choosing a propeller with a different pitch.

For props that fail to provide the recommended rpm, correct the difference with a pitch variation of 1-inch for every 200 rpm of variance. For example, if the WOT reading is 400 rpms less than recommended, select a prop with 2 inches less pitch. If the reading is 400 rpms more, choose

a prop with 2 inches more pitch.

The ProPulse patented adjustable pitch composite propeller from InterCon Marketing, has an adjustable pitch feature that allows the bass boater to quickly adjust the pitch of the ProPulse's replaceable blades. The four blades can be set at five different positions, theoretically increasing or decreasing engine output by 400 rpm. In just a few minutes, you can optimize engine performance and improve boat speed and handling.

Prop Design

Props, however can get a bit more complicated. High performance props on bass boats often feature rake and cup. Rake is the angle of a blade in relation to the outer hub. High rake angles give the blades a "leaned" back look with the trailing edge of the blades extending beyond the back of the hub.

Rake also reduces problems with ventilation, which occurs when air bubbles appear in the water around the prop, robbing the blades of their thrusting power. Naturally, ventilation happens in situations that bring surface air close to the prop. That means that boaters who run in choppy water, make sharp turns or have highly-positioned motors, may increase performance by using a raked prop.

Cupped props feature blades with trailing edges that curl away from the boat. The last one-half inch or so of each blade may bend

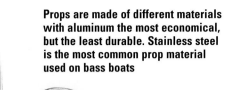

Props are made of different materials with aluminum the most economical, but the least durable. Stainless steel is the most common prop material used on bass boats

away suddenly, somewhat like a flap on the end of an airplane wing.

Both of these prop features can sometimes improve performance on bass boats. They essentially provide additional bow lift for fast boats with highly-positioned outboards. More lift means less of the hull drags over the water, and that improves both acceleration and top-end performance. These types of performance props, however, are quite expensive, and unless gaining a mile per hour in speed is important, they aren't really necessary for most bass boaters.

High-Performance Props

Bass boaters looking for the ultimate in prop tuning may consider some other prop designs including chopper and cleaver style props. Chopper props feature long, narrow blades that are extremely swept or raked back. They can provide more bow lift and higher top-end speeds. Cleaver props feature straight trailing edges with extremely sharp points at the blade tips. Clever props create a great deal of stern lift and are primarily used in tunnel hull offshore boats. Cleaver props are not normally recommended for use on bass boats.

Blade Numbers

Bass boaters can improve performance-

by installing a prop with more blades. An extra blade can provide additional "bite" in the water, for better power and acceleration. Four-blade props are very efficient when getting on plane because there are more blades in the water at once. They significantly reduce

cavitation during turns and improve rough-water handling and control. A four-blade prop is most efficient in mid-range throttle settings and a bass boater can pick up two to four miles per hour as the prop brings the slip factor down. In high-range, however, four-blade props seem to lose performance, perhaps because they create additional drag.

Five- and six-blade props are also available on the market. These multi-blade props can significantly increase performance and handling when combined with high-mounted motor applications. Higher engine mounts reduce drag; therefore, multi-blade props allow the use of higher pitches, which can let the engine develop more rpm and increase speed. Five-bladed props, for example, are well suited to extremely heavy applications or in high engine situations.

Props with more blades turn with less vibration, but create more drag. For instance, four-blade props don't turn as fast as three-blade props. If you are planning to increase blade numbers, you should consider reducing pitch by 1 inch for each blade added. If you use a jackplate, the extra height reduces the drag on the lower unit and the extra prop blades help maintain water contact. The result can be a higher top end, but retaining better out-of-the-hole acceleration. Four-,

Jackplates set the engine back away from the transom and can add to a bass boat's performance.

five-, and six-blade props do not have as much prop slip, especially at the lower speeds. A major consideration, however, is whether the engine has enough torque to handle the extra blades and turn them into better performance.

Prop Materials

Props are available in a range of materials, the most common being aluminum, stainless steel, or plastic composite. Aluminum props have the advantage of being lightweight and inexpensive but are easily damaged. Plastic composite props are also lightweight and corrosion-free, but most have about the same durability range as aluminum. Stainless-steel props are more sturdy but much more expensive. Stainless-steel props are most commonly used on high-performance bass boats. Super-durable titanium props are also available for those who wish to spend the money.

As you can see, selecting the correct prop for your bass boat can be somewhat complicated. You should work with a marine dealer when selecting a prop. Dealers can explain how to find out if an existing prop is providing maximum performance and some dealers even allow bass boaters to test new props in the water. This is usually done with the understanding that "if you ding it, you buy it." The dealer will generally take back a prop if you are not satisfied, but the prop must be free of defects.

JACKPLATES

The jackplate, a mechanical engine mount fastened to the boat's transom, provides an easy method of positioning the engine to maximize the propeller's efficiency. Jackplates allow you to raise and lower the engine in pre-

Types of Jackplates

Fixed Jackplate

Fixed, nonadjustable, jackplates allow the engine to be bolted permanently in one position.

Hydraulic Jackplate

Can be adjusted while running, to lower the engine for hole-shots, raise it for greater speed, or adjust to navigate shallow water.

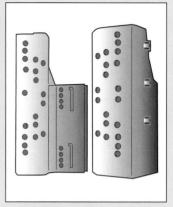

Jackplate SetBack

Jackplates are available in a variety of "set backs," or distances they set the engine from the transom.

cise increments to attain the best handling characteristics for your boat. They also provide "setback" which gets the prop away from the water turbulence and gives the prop a better "bite." Setback also gives the motor leverage to get the bow of the boat up using less trim. Models are available with setbacks, ranging from 5 to 14 inches.

In theory every outboard powered boat could benefit from a jackplate, but for the most part, jackplates are normally used only on larger boats and by boaters who require greater performance from their bass boats. Jackplates are available, however, for motors as small as 35 horsepower.

Jackplates come with either manual or electric hydraulic adjustment. Manual jackplates use either a screw or ratchet adjustment to

raise or lower the engine. The engine stays fixed in that position until the screw or ratchet is turned again. This allows for some pretty finite tuning of the engine height. Several years ago David Greenwood of Suzuki Marine helped with a boat test on a Challenger bass boat, rigged with a Suzuki 150 horsepower motor and a manual jackplate. With the jackplate, David was able to raise the engine in 1/6-inch increments until he achieved the desired result. When we finished, I could literally drive the boat with my fingertips at well over 60 mph.

Hydraulic systems allow you to adjust the jackplate with your fingertips while under way and work independently of the power tilt and trim. This provides the ultimate in control because you can instantly

adjust to changing water conditions.

Jackplates also take the chine walk out of some boats, because the motor doesn't have to be trimmed out as far to produce higher speeds. In rough water, having the capability of lowering your motor can give you a better "bite" with the prop, eliminating cavitation. Different loads, different water conditions and different speeds will dictate where your prop should be to provide the best performance.

Basically the less motor that is in the water, the faster the boat will go. When the motor is higher, your engine works less to maintain speed because there is less drag. This means improved fuel economy as well as longer engine life. In shallow water a hydraulic jackplate can be used to raise the motor, keeping the prop level. This is more efficient than using the tilt to keep the prop from hitting the bottom because it makes the boat easier to steer when the motor is raised vertically instead of tilting.

Cook Manufacturing Corporation has been marketing jackplates since 1985. Rick Presley, Cook's Vice President, explains the value of jackplates this way. "Set back gets the prop of the engine back away from the transom and water turbulence and into what is called "cleaner water. This gives the prop a better "bite" at a higher prop setting eliminating prop slippage. Set back also gives the motor leverage to get the bow to rise, the more efficiently the engine pushes the boat through the water. The less the engine has to be trimmed out to get the bow to rise, the more efficiently the boat pushes the boat through the water. Our standard unit has a 5 1/2-inch set back and that's the ultimate set back on the majority of the boats on the market. Some boats that are extremely bow heavy could benefit from a larger set back."

If you plan to mount a jackplate, you should also install a water-pressure gauge. This is the best protection against overheating your motor with a too-high motor location. The gauge will let you determine if the water pressure drops below the psi recommended by the motor manufacturer. You should also consider gauges that indicate the height of the engine. Most jackplate manufacturers offer one and a universal model is available from Panther Marine.

Installation

Jackplate installation is not particularly difficult, but will require a chain hoist and heavy support to lift the motor. Before installing a jackplate be sure that the boat transom will support the installation. A jackplate places additional weight and torque on the transom.

1. **Remove the cowling** and fly-wheel cover from the engine and mount a lifting bolt to the engine.

2. **Using a chain hoist, lift the engine** slightly to ease tension on the engine bolts. Remove the engine-mounting bolts. This is best done with two people, one working inside the motor well and one outside.

3. **Lift the engine** and swing it away from the boat, (or move the boat away from the suspended engine).

4. **Cut the old seal away** from the transom, using a razor-blade window scraper. Be careful not to cut or scar the transom area outside the engine-mounting location. Apply a good amount of fresh marine silicone sealant to the holes from the original motor mount.

5. **Attach the jackplate** to the transom following the manufacturer's instructions. Use the original motor-mounting bolts provided. You may need to install additional washers.

Chapter 4

Trolling Motors

One element in design that has set bass boats apart from other fishing craft is the placement of an electric trolling motor on the bow. This allows the angler to precisely maneuver the bass boat while casting from the bow platform.

"**W**orld went to pot when they put the 'gol dang' trolling motor on the front of the boat," said an old-time river guide a number of years ago. Unfortunately, he was against change. Fortunately, trolling motor manufacturers are not. My old-time guide friend is probably rolling over in his grave at the wonders of bow-mounted trolling motors.

The major feature that sets bass boats apart from other fishing boats are bow-mount trolling motors. Placing the trolling motor on the bow offers several advantages to bass anglers. The motor pulls the boat rather than pushing it, allowing for more precise maneuvering. Since bass angling is mostly casting, having an elevated casting platform at the bow of a bass boat provides for excellent visibility and easy casting, flipping, and pitching. Bow-mounted trolling motors allow for hands-free navigating; hence the angler can concentrate on casting and retrieving rather than managing the motor. This is accomplished by either a foot pedal or by using an extended arm moved by the angler's knee or foot.

Bow-mounts also provide a place to position an LCD transducer. In the past, these were simply clamped onto the motor with the cable running up the outside of the motor shaft to the LCD. Pinpoint trolling motors have transducers built into the motor housing, eliminating the need for running the exterior cable and also the possibility of hanging it up on an obstacle.

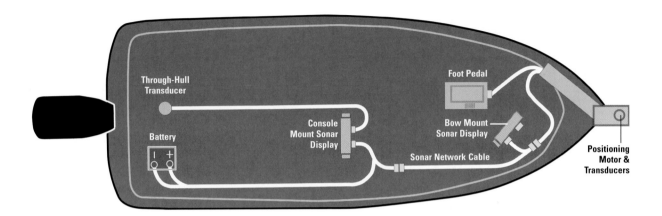

Through-Hull Transducer

Battery

Console Mount Sonar Display

Foot Pedal

Bow Mount Sonar Display

Sonar Network Cable

Positioning Motor & Transducers

CHOOSING BOW-MOUNT TROLLING MOTORS

It is important to choose the correct trolling motor to match your boat size and fishing techniques. In many "package" boats, the trolling motor is selected to compliment the boat. You may, however, wish to choose a different motor or consider an upgrade. In this case, the first step is to determine the minimum/maximum shaft length you will need. The height from the top of the deck to the waterline varies from bass boat to bass boat. It's important that the trolling motor propeller be positioned adequately below the waterline.

This may vary according to wind and wave conditions causing the boat to rock and roll. A trolling motor shaft that is too short will bring the prop out of the water when the bow rises. To realize maximum performance the prop should be approximately 3 to 4 inches below the water line.

While this depth can be adjusted to some degree by the adjustment knob on the trolling motor mount, some bass boats with deeper V bows require a fairly long shaft. On average, bass boats 18 feet and under will require the standard 41-inch-shaft trolling motor. Boats 19 feet and longer require a 45-inch shaft. There are also 50- and 60-inch shafts for deeper V boats.

If you choose a larger motor, you'll need multiple batteries to operate not only the trolling motor but also the electronics, bilge pump, and livewell pump as well. Trolling motors are available as 12V (one- battery), 12/24V (one- or two-battery), 24V (one-battery), 24/36V (two- or three-battery) or 36V (three-battery) systems. Larger bass boats do best with multiple-battery systems — going to a 24-volt system will almost double the pounds of thrust but will consume about the same amps as a 12-volt system powering a high-thrust motor. If

you're a serious tournament angler, or are going to be fishing hard all day in a heavy boat, a 24- or even 36-volt system not only provides more power but also uses less amps to do so.

Compare
Facts about Thrust

Minimum thrust:

BOAT LENGTH	THRUST IN POUNDS
Aluminum John boats: 14 to 15 feet	27 to 30 lbs
Aluminum boats: 16 to 17 feet	40 lbs
Aluminum boats: 18 to 20 feet	50 to 60 lbs
Fiberglass boats: 16 to 18 feet	70 lbs
Fiberglass boats: 19 to 20 feet	100 lbs

Installing Bow-Mount Trolling Motors

1. Read the manufacturer's installation book and make sure you have everything on hand to install the motor. The types of hardware needed to mount the motor depends on whether you fish in demanding environments, such as rough water, stump fields or other situations that may cause the motor to come loose, or in less demanding situations.

2. Determine whether there is accessibility to the underside of the bow gunwale. For operation under relatively calm conditions, or if there is no access to the underside of the bow gunwale, molded rubber isolators with threaded inserts can be placed through the mount base holes bored in the deck. They work in the same manner as wall mollies for anchoring things to sheetrock walls.

3. If access is available to the underside of the bow and you will use the motor in demanding conditions, bolts with washers and locknuts should be used.

4. On most units, especially those with a spring-loaded breakaway bracket, it's important to position the outer end of the bracket 3 inches, or whatever is recommended by the manufacturer, out over the edge of the bow gunwale. This provides clearance for the motor to swing back when it strikes an obstacle.

5. Make sure that the control head has proper clearance on your deck when in the down or stowed position. The motor should be located with the head high enough above the deck so that it can be properly secured when stowed. The head should not be able to slap against the deck when running in rough water.

6. Once you've located the proper position, mark, and then bore the holes through the gunwale and install in place.

7. If the motor utilizes a foot control, it can be positioned where it's most comfortable for you to use and permanently mounted or simply left loose if desired. Some Minn Kota trolling motors feature an extremely long cord on the foot control, allowing you to work the trolling motor from any position in the boat. Also, you may wish to leave the foot control loose in case you change seat types.

The next step is to choose the features you desire. Following are some of the top motors and their main features.

TROLLING MOTORS

Minn Kota AutoPilot

- AutoPilot automatic steering system.
- Grip Glide system (PowerDrive and AutoPilot) allows the angler to easily unlock the stowed motor and lower it into the water or raise it back into the stowed position. An automatic stow and trim feature is also available.
- Impact Protection system uses a swing-away spring mount and non-corrosive flexible composite shaft.
- Weedless Wedge swept-back prop blades that "wedge" weeds away from the hub.

MotorGuide

- Improved armature winding and wire diameter designed to create greater thrust in smaller units.
- Stow/run switch on the pedal that puts unit in the appropriate stow or run position.
- Servo-positioning steering. The lower unit and control pedal are attached with a "virtual" cable. For each pedal position there is a corresponding lower unit position (boat position).
- Gator-II sprig-arm breakaway mount.
- Stainless steel shaft.

TRANSOM MOUNTED TROLLING MOTORS

Although bow-mount trolling motors have become increasingly popular, transom-mounted models are still the main event for many fishing situations and boat styles. A wide range of selections is available if your boat and fishing method requires a transom mount. MotorGuide has 15 models available for freshwater fishing ranging from 22 to 107 pounds of thrust. Minn Kota carries 22 models ranging from 30 to 101 pounds of thrust. Evinrude has two models in the Scout series with thrust-pounds of 30 and 40 and their Seaquest line carries models with 36, 70, and 74 pounds of thrust.

Minn Kota Maxxum, 50T (12 volt) and 74T (24 volt)

- "Cool Power" system.
- "Maximizer" solid-state circuitry.
- Variable speed control.
- Battery charge indicator with test button.
- Two-blade "Weedless Wedge" prop.
- Composite shaft.
- Tilt twist mounting bracket-

Minn Kota Auto Pilot motors offer automatic steering that locks the motor on to a compass heading to keep your boat on course.

FISHING WITH A PINPOINT SYSTEM

I've had a Charger bass boat rigged with a Pinpoint Positioning System since they have been available and I have found that each generation of motor has become better. For those anglers who might have been on the other side of the moon in recent years, the Pinpoint Positioning System consists of a trolling motor with built-in transducers connected to a mini-computer contained in the trolling motor head. The transducers and mini-computer automatically guide the boat. Two different models are available. The 2000 Model has one transducer to create a bottom-tracking mode. Set the depth you want to follow or stay in into the system and the motor will track that depth. The 3000 Series motors have five transducers. They allow the unit to scan the bottom, to the sides, and to follow a shoreline or underwater feature.

The trolling motor is not the only part of the system. The new Pinpoint Network System integrates fishing electronics, trolling motor, and fish finders, allowing them to work together without interfering with each other. Pinpoint Sonar Imaging displays offer two units. A bow mount plugs directly into the trolling motor and uses its transducers to allow you to see images from the bow casting deck while fishing. A second unit – in-dash or

- lever-lock or push button.
- Multi-position tiller handle.
- Universal Sonar (option). LCDs plug into the trolling motor.

Evinrude models Scout 40H (12 volt) and Seaquest 74H (24 volt)
- Offset anodized aluminum shaft (composite shafts available on some models).
- All-metal 10-position tilt mounting bracket.
- Speed control: Scout 40H five-forward, three-reverse; Seaquest 74H variable- speed motor.
- Electronic speed control and "SilentStart" (Seaquest 74H).
- Weedless prop.

MotorGuide Energy Transom ET54V and ET76V
- WideBite transom mount (3-1/4-inch maximum opening).
- Chrome steel shaft (ET54V 36-inch and ET76V 42-inch).
- Three-blade Machete II prop.
- Variable speed forward/reverse twist-tiller handle.
- Master switch under the head.

The pedal position on this MotorGuide trolling motor controls the boat's course leaving the angler's hands free for casting.

Trolling Motors

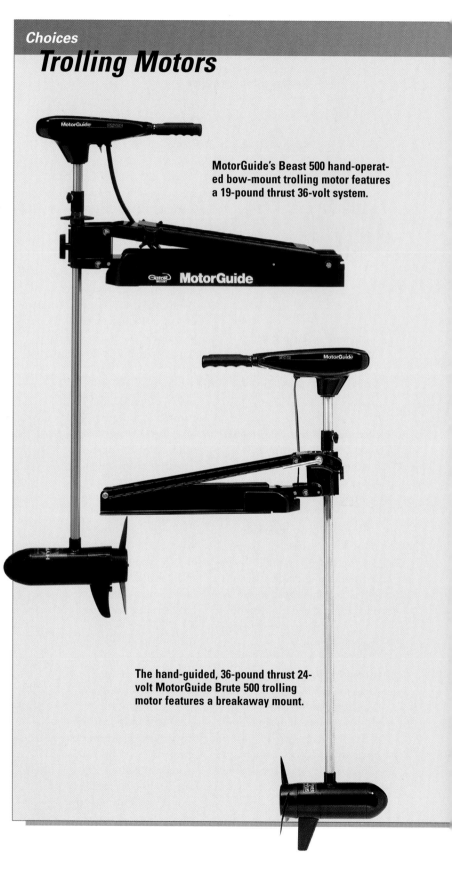

stand-alone – is connected to a separate transducer located on the transom or in the bilge area. This provides the best of both worlds; the ability to view from the driver's seat while scouting for fish or watch the bow unit while casting or drift fishing. The dash unit can be used while trolling or viewed by a partner on the back deck.

By hooking the two units together with an auxiliary console-to-bow "Y" cable, you can split the screen on either sonar to view information coming from both the bow and transom transducers. Using the motors and LCDs in conjunction is extremely effective. All Pinpoint Sonar Imaging displays are Pinpoint network compatible and plug directly into any Pinpoint Positioning Motor or select MotorGuide trolling motors (with built-in transducers).

I began testing the Pinpoints with the original 5-transducer motor and still prefer it because of its versatility, but the 2000 Series does offer the most popular tracking routine, depth tracking, and a much lower cost than the 5-transducer motor. "We offered depth track because most gamefish relate to specific depths at various times of the year," said Dallas Hodges, Pinpoint's director of marketing. "Our pros are just beginning to realize the benefits of being able to accurately track specific depth contours and locate schools of fish positioned on structure. The key to using the System as a fishing tool is learning how to

MotorGuide's Beast 500 hand-operated bow-mount trolling motor features a 19-pound thrust 36-volt system.

The hand-guided, 36-pound thrust 24-volt MotorGuide Brute 500 trolling motor features a breakaway mount.

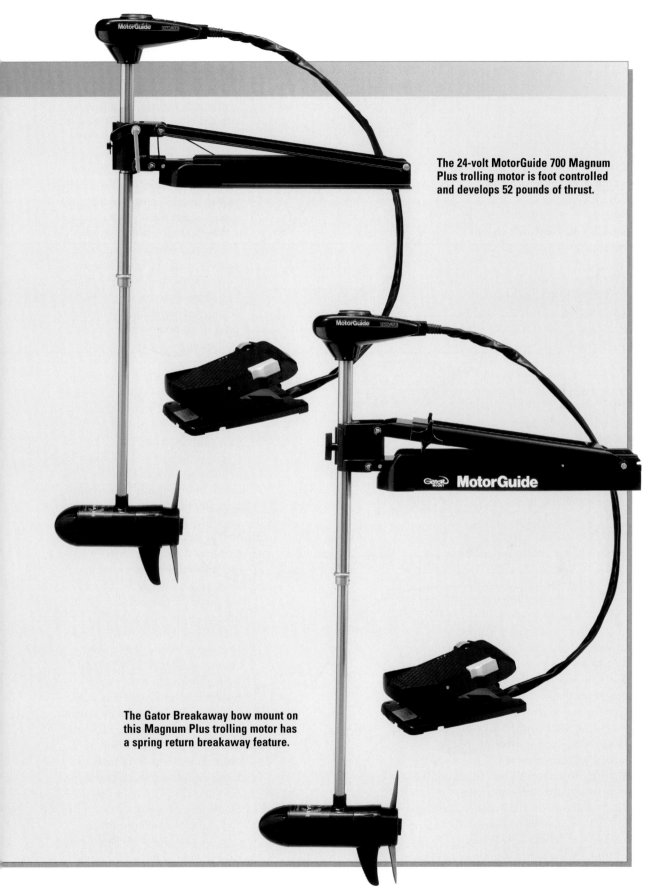

The 24-volt MotorGuide 700 Magnum Plus trolling motor is foot controlled and develops 52 pounds of thrust.

The Gator Breakaway bow mount on this Magnum Plus trolling motor has a spring return breakaway feature.

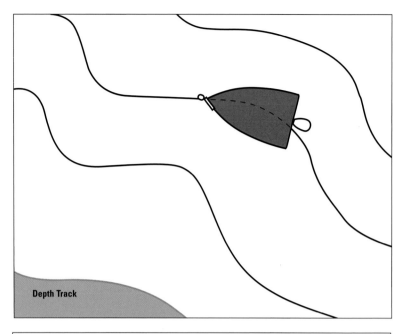

Depth Track

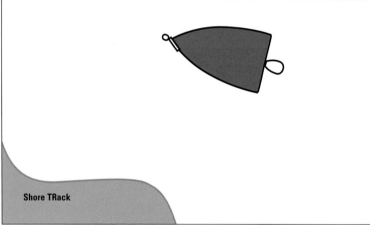

Shore TRack

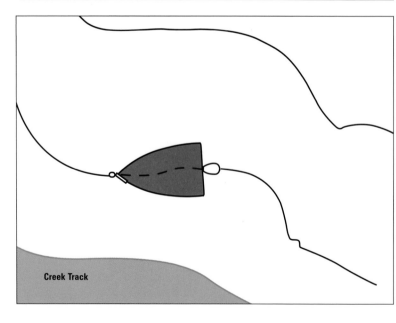

Creek Track

Pinpoint Positioning Motors function in three modes. Depth track, which follows a set depth, shore track, which locks onto the shore or weed line, and creek track, which follows contours or features on the bottom.

let it hunt out and show you subtle break lines, like small cuts and points, the first time you fish a piece of structure."

One of the first times I used the Pinpoint Positioning Motor was on Stockton Lake, near my home in Missouri, where summer bass locate at a specific depth. I found that automatically following a depth contour was much easier than using a foot-control while watching a depth finder. When I caught a fish, I just let the motor continue to run while I unhooked the fish. When I returned to fishing, I was still on the magic 22-foot contour, hassle free. Upon reaching the end of a fishing area, a simple touch of a switch and the motor automatically steered my boat 180 degrees to cover the area from the opposite direction.

The depth track does have a problem. When you follow a contour that runs out to an abrupt drop-off say, along a flat to a submerged river channel the system becomes confused. I did discover, as Dallas mentioned, lots of little cuts and pockets I didn't realize existed, and on a lake I've been fishing for many years. Depth tracking is also a great way of fishing a hump, reef, or flooded island by simply setting the depth to the location of the fish spotted on the sonar. Another great tactic is to hover with depth track over a specific structure such as a rock pile on the end of a point.

I also like the Shore Track capability on the 3000 Series but have found it a bit more complicated. The makeup of a shoreline has a lot to do with the tracking capability. Extremely shallow flats are the hardest, bluffs the easiest. The unit will follow the contour exactly where it can read it properly. Vegetation can create a problem; the motor will follow the edge of a major weed bed as if it were a shoreline. You also have to watch out for stumps and especially "widow-maker" snags, steering around them manually. Simply touch the "momentary" button on the foot pedal, steer around the obstacle, and press the "Resume" button to continue. Shoreline tracking is particularly useful for night fishing. Simply set a distance and let the motor do the navigating while you concentrate on your fishing.

The third mode is the most interesting. Creek track uses the transducers to follow a break such as a submerged creek or river channel, ledge, or other structure. This is a great way to fish for bass during summer and winter when they may be holding just off the edge of a feature. I like to make a pass following the channel and use buoys to mark stumps, rock piles, and fishing features such as small cuts and other structures.

An important element in all these tactics is to maintain the speed against wind or current to

Bass Boat Facts
Bow Trolling Motor Mounts

Some of the handiest new mounting devices are the on/off motor mounts that allow you to remove a trolling motor within seconds to prevent theft when the boat is not in use, or if your bass boat doubles as a pleasure boat for the family. Most mounts can be installed with marine stainless steel self-tapping screws.

- Bass Pro – Quick-Release Scissors Mount designed for Minn Kota.

- Removable Trolling Motor Bracket – Fits all Minn Kota 700 and 800 series Power Drive and Autopilots, Deckhand Anchors, and all MotorGuide bow mount motors except Gator Motors.

- Ultimate Trolling Motor Mount - Fully retractable and removable model for Minn Kota and MotorGuide motors.

allow the motor to properly control the boat. If the speed is not fast enough, the wind or current tends to push the boat around, causing the tracking modes to work harder to regain their proper positions. Speed should also be suited to the tactic. For the trolling motor to track efficiently, it is important to keep the main motor down and straight.

One of the features of the Pinpoint system that I liked was the system software that enables you to fine-tune the operation of the motor. For instance, the Automatic Speed Control (ASC)

allows you to set up your motor to accommodate the actual fishing conditions. This allows the Pinpoint Motor to ramp up its speed when a gust of wind blows the boat off course and acts to keep the depth tracking system on target. All 3000 Series motors have a large, easy to use keypad. The digital depth and temperature displays are large and easy to see and the battery strength is indicated on the keypad. When equipped with a trolling motor plug and matching bow plug, the motor can be removed or installed in a matter of seconds.

Chapter 5

Electronics

An angler adjusts his console mounted fish-finding display. Electronics are a major feature on bass boats, and the fully rigged boat may have as many as six units.

When Carl Lowrance introduced his little green box in 1957, everything in the fishing world changed. Though crude compared to today's high-tech models, the flasher showed anglers what was under the water and quickly became a standard item with bass anglers, especially tournament anglers. As his "fish finder" became more popular, Lowrance went one better and introduced the paper-chart fish finder. I was fortunate to go to Scotland during the Lowrance-sponsored Operation Deepscan hunt for the Loch Ness monster in 1987. Not only did this bring attention to the world of "fish finders" it was a lot of fun. "Now I 'cotch 'em all," said one old-time fishing guide on the loch. I tried to explain that just because he could see the marks of fish, he certainly wouldn't be able to catch them all.

I have used both flashers and chart recorders for many years, and although many new products are on the market, flashers are still popular with bass anglers. These days, bass boat electronics consist of several different devices, including liquid crystal displays (LCDs), liquid crystal graphs (LCGs), global positioning systems (GPS) and/or chart plotters, and speed and water temperature gauges. Some units combine fish-finding capabilities with GPS and chart plotting.

The fully equipped bass boat will have several electronic units. I actually run four on my Charger bass boat. The first is an in-dash flasher. This provides instant information on depth as I run up on plane, or even when scouting at slower speeds. On the console is an LCD, equipped with GPS. When it comes time for a detailed look, the console LCD provides the answers. It reveals the bottom and structure, as well as showing schools of baitfish and even bass. The bow holds an LCD – a Pinpoint – that uses the transducers in the trolling motor.

FLASHERS

You can't beat flashers for real-time viewing, a good reason for using them for high-speed navigation. Some anglers, especially shallow-water aficionados, prefer their real-time feature for bow-mount electronics. For this reason, most bass boat makers leave an opening or round cutout for a flasher in the bow of their boats. Flashers provide just as much information as LCDs, but are harder for some anglers to interpret.

LIQUID CRYSTAL DISPLAY SONARS

The most popular and commonly used electronics are liquid crystal displays. These are available in a wide range of prices with a variety of different features. For the most part, all of these units work in the same way. A transducer provides depth and object information to a computer that then translates the information onto a

liquid crystal screen. The image on the screen is produced by tiny squares called pixels. The number of pixels in the screen is one of the main differences in units. The more pixels available, the better the definition the screen will show. This is important when trying to separate fish from structure.

One method of determining the degree of detail is to divide the number of vertical pixels of the unit into the range or water depth in which the unit will be most commonly used. For instance, dividing a 120-pixel screen into 60 feet would result in two pixels per foot. One pixel per 6 inches doesn't provide a lot of detail when it comes to separating fish from the bottom or structure. Hence a 240-pixel unit will provide twice the detail and separation. Some units are marketed with pixels described vertically and horizontally, others listed by pixels per square inch. Some of the better and more expensive units have several thousand pixels per square inch.

CATHODE RAY TUBE SONARS

Another type of sonar uses a cathode ray tube (CRT) display. These are primarily used for saltwater angling and by some walleye pros. CRT, or videosonar, does have some advantages. Information is almost instantaneous from the sonar to screen and the screen can

be viewed from almost any angle, whereas an LCD screen must be viewed pretty well from head-on. CRT screens tend to wash out in sunlight and are primarily used in covered boats, (one bass pro I know has a CRT located under his console). The color screens of CRTs provide better differentiation between objects displayed on the screen.

DIGITAL DEPTH FINDERS

Digital depth finders are normally mounted in the dash and primarily used for navigation. They give a constant readout of water depth in number form. They do not pro-

Flasher units offer real-time viewing and are often used on the console to provide navigation information and for fast "scouting" of structure.

A temperature gauge is extremely important. Digital dash mounts are extremely popular, with the sensor mounted on the transom.

to see the display while out of the water and practice with the menu. Backlighted display is a feature that makes it easier to view the screen during night and periods of low visibility.

ZOOM

An important feature to look for in a fish finder is zoom. In zoom mode the bottom area is magnified, offering greater detail. This is important when you want to separate fish signals from the bottom structure. Even most of the more economical models offer the zoom feature; however, they normally display the zoom view as a full screen, meaning you either have to view in zoom or on the normal viewing screen. The better units offer a split screen with a zoom feature on one side and the standard view on the other. With the split screen you can view the enlarged detail of the bottom on one side of the screen and monitor the entire water column on the other.

Screens are either square or a vertical or horizontal rectangle. A factor to consider if you use the zoom feature often is to choose a screen that is a horizontal rectangle. If you do not use the zoom feature regularly, a vertical rectangle screen provides better target separation and detail because more pixels are displayed in each vertical column. With 240 pixels at 4X zoom, each pixel will represent about ¾ inch.

vide secondary information about fish or bait schools that the flashers provide.

TEMPERATURE GAUGES

One of the handiest devices you can own is a simple in-dash temperature gauge. This provides constant temperature readings from a sensor mounted on the lower part of the boat's transom. At certain times of the year, in early spring for instance when you're looking for the warmest water, these little units can be invaluable. I keep my temperature gauge running all the time when I'm in the boat.

FISH FINDER FEATURES

Following are several of the features available. Many units have a built-in simulator that allows you

ALARMS AND IDS

Fish ID and fish alarms are features available on some units. In fish ID, signals that could be fish are identified. Some models also indicate the depth of the readings. One thing to remember, however, is when this feature is in operation the screen tends to have less sensitivity. Unfortunately, weeds, tips of branches, and other underwater objects also often show up as fish IDs. For the most part, you're better off turning this feature off. Fish alarms are available that beep when the sonar beam contacts a fish target. Many units have depth alarms that can be set to sound when a certain depth is attained.

MEMORY

Some of the better fish finders have a memory function that allows you to recall a specific number of scenes. Even better are liquid crystal recorders (LCRs), which permit you to record and store readouts. Lowrance and Pinpoint use tiny memory cards to store hours of screen readouts. You can recall the readouts for review and even download them onto a personal computer.

One of the most interesting aspects of the Pinpoint system is their ViewSaver, an accessory that links Pinpoint sonar imaging displays to a personal computer. This feature can greatly increase your knowledge of your favorite lake. ViewSaver allows you to download up to six on-the-water views from a Pinpoint sonar display onto a PC's hard drive for cataloging and storage. You can transfer any bit-mapped image or text document back onto the Pinpoint display screen. These files might include a bit-mapped lake map, a list of important lake contacts, phone numbers, or even a custom table that includes the minimum size, slot limits and other catch restrictions for each lake fished.

GRAY TONES

LCDs show sonar echoes on the screen in tones of black (or other single color) only on the more economical units. Better units use up to 10 different color tones. The weakest signals will be shown as the lightest shades of gray; the strongest signals as the darkest. Units with more shades of gray, now called LCGs, or liquid crystal graphs, make it easier to delineate between echoes, to distinguish fish from underwater weeds. Upper scale sonar LCGs are available with color instead of the monochrome screens. Color provides the highest definition since tar-gets are indicated by specific colors depending on the sonar return.

GRAYLINE

Most units have a bottom-reading feature called "grayline." This reveals the composition of the bottom. The difference between a hard and a soft bottom is seen on the screen as a gray line. Since hard objects produce a stronger signal, softer bottoms show as a

Zoom is one of the most popular LCG features. The split screen allows you to see the entire water column, and also zoom in on the bottom for more detail.

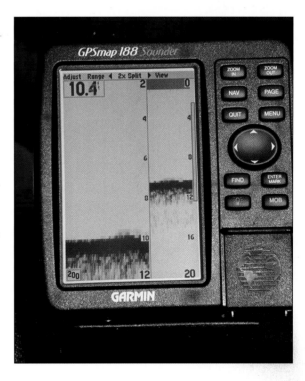

A wide variety of transducer designs are available. Those with two-beam coverage can be set for shallow or deeper water.

Most sonar units employ a single beam providing a fixed degree of coverage. Others have the capability of switching between two beams. For instance, a standard 20-degree beam is used for maximum definition in moderate to deep water while a beam with wider coverage is used in shallow water.

Other transducers offer triple beams to provide more coverage around the boat. Transducers with multiple beams allow you to scan down, out, and even sideways. The latter are important in extremely shallow water and when fishing weed beds, brush, or under docks; 3-D view, available in some sonar units, provides a three-dimensional underwater view that resembles a topographical map.

SCREEN SPEED

There is a delayed response between the time the transducer receives a signal and the time the information is displayed on the screen. LCDs and LCGs do not provide instant information, although some newer units are able to scan as fast as 40 pixels per second. Even so, you're not seeing information displayed on the screen in real time when you are speeding across a lake. For this reason, many of the upper-end units offer a flasher bar or chart feature that can be set up on the screen. These "real-time" readouts maximize transmission bursts, with speeds of 60 pixels per second or higher. Despite these advances they still provide slower readouts than a true flasher.

RANGE

The depth range features available to bass anglers vary considerably among units produced by different manufacturers. The maximum depth range tends to vary from just over 100 to more than 1,000 feet. Most units offer automatic range selection for depth. Others come with manual capability to set specific depth ranges. This can be a valuable feature for anglers who fish in shallow water. With the fish finder set on automatic function, the unit will show the appropriate depth-range display on the screen. Units with two-beam coverage are more versatile.

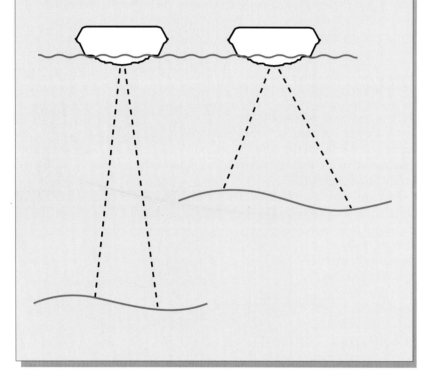

thin gray line while hard bottoms show as a wider band.

Proper adjustment of the grayline is extremely important when you're trying to determine the composition of the bottom or pick features off the bottom. The first step is to adjust the sensitivity and then adjust the grayline to

provide a band reading which shows half of the bottom gray and the lower half black. A problem occurs over weed beds. Weed beds often give a strong return signal which is shown as a wide grayline on the screen. It is often necessary to reduce the unit's sensitivity when over dense vegetation.

USING ELECTRONICS

LCGs and LCDs are available with numerous programs, menus and features, depending on the unit. All features can be operated in automatic mode and usually work just fine for most typical fishing situations. Automatic settings such as range, chart speed, and contrast are adjustable on some models. Different units also offer a wide variety of manual programming choices to customize your sonar view to your particular fishing style or needs. Manual programming simply gets the most from the unit.

Setting proper sensitivity is the most important factor. The more density an object has, the stronger the echo that bounces back from it. Weeds being less dense than wood, for instance, will produce a weaker echo than a stump or log. Very dense objects such as rocks will produce an even stronger return. Objects of the same density but of different sizes return dissimilar echoes as well. This means that large bass will reflect a stronger echo than small bass. The stronger the signal, the thicker the marks presented on the screen. When the signal from your transducer passes over a stationary fish the return signal is displayed as an arch on your screen. When your transducer's signal first strikes the fish, the distance the sound travels to the fish is greater than the distance when your transducer is directly over the fish. As the transducer passes the fish, the distance

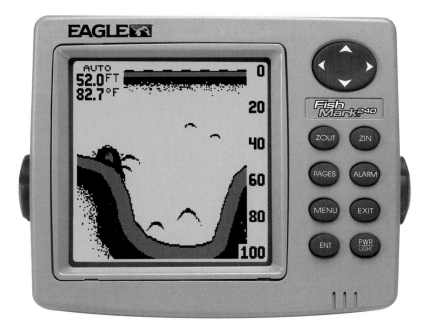

the sound must travel again increases. This creates the arched image on the screen.

Fish arches display best when the boat is moving at a speed of only a few miles per hour and in water at least 10 feet deep. At really slow fishing speeds, some extremely fast-scrolling units will show the fish signal as flat rather than arched because the transducer is over the fish for a much longer period of time. The best way of ensuring seeing fish arches in this case is to keep your sensitivity as high as possible.

Higher sensitivity can allow you to spot a thermocline, a layer of water in a thermally stratified lake. Lower sensitivity, on the other hand, provides a better overall look at targets and gives a better view of the bottom. It's extremely important to keep the

sensitivity setting consistent. Typically, the best sensitivity level shows a good, solid bottom signal with grayline. A good method of setting sensitivity is to turn the sensitivity setting up until the screen contains a series of random dots and adjust the setting back down slightly.

GLOBAL POSITIONING SYSTEMS

Global positioning systems, or GPSs, have been increasingly popular with saltwater and walleye pros for the simple reason that GPS allows them to relocate good fishing spots in open water. As more bass anglers discover "offshore" bass fishing, the use of GPS has increased. GPS units can range in cost from just a few hundred

When mounting a transducer screen on a console or gunwale, it is important to make sure that nothing obstructs the tilting action of the mount, and that the screen is easily visible.

dollars up to several thousand, depending on the size and features.

GPS is available both in small hand-held units as well as permanent-mount units. Portable units perform well for many location and navigation chores. They are economical and take up less space in the boat. Since managing a hand-held unit is difficult while driving a boat, several companies make simple GPS mounts. These permit the GPS unit to be easily removed for other purposes such as hunting or hiking. A fixed mount on the other hand allows for a bigger screen with more menus and options. Permanently mounted GPS units will require an external antenna – more electronics and yet another item on your boat. GPS units are available as stand-alone units or as an integral part of a sonar unit.

Many GPSs and combination sonar/GPS units offer the advantage of chart plotting – a digital chart or map on the screen. Most provide a built-in background map, but, because they cover a wide area, do not offer great detail. They also can't be changed or enhanced. A second type of chart is available on a CD-Rom or map cartridge. These generally

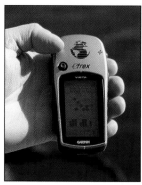

A permanently mounted GPS unit offers a larger screen and other convenient marine features. Many GPS units come combined with sonar systems.

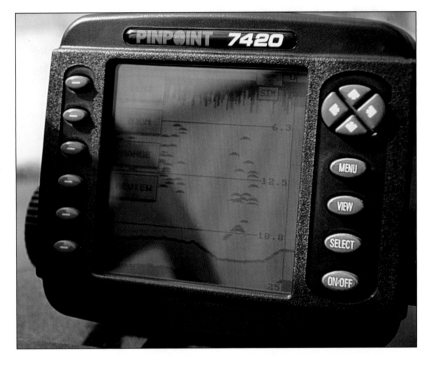

This transducer from Pinpoint provides, speed, wheel position, and temperature readouts.

cover one lake or waterway. In the case of large bodies of water they may cover small sections. The maps are not interchangeable between units and must be matched to the proper brand of plotter. These maps provide the greatest amount of detail, and you can add your own information on some, marking fishing hot spots or underwater obstacles. The GPS portion of the maps provides running longitude and latitude, with instant GPS waypoints and the ability to plot, name, make notes, and save for future reference.

WIDE AREA AUGMENTATION SYSTEM

The first GPS systems were satellite-directed and their accuracy wasn't particularly good. The more accurate differential GPS (DGPS) uses ground stations for position correction, and while it offers greater accuracy to bass boaters, the system primarily benefits navigation on bigger waters.

Raytheon's Wide Area Augmentation System (WAAS) uses a master station that computes and corrects errors before sending the information to satellites, one located over the West Coast and one over the East Coast. The satellites beam the corrected information to your GPS. Raytheon has estimated that standard GPS accuracy is within 60 feet. DGPS has an accuracy of around 30 feet and WAAS accuracy ranges to 10 feet and under. If extreme accuracy is important, you may wish to consider a GPS unit using the WAAS or a unit that can be upgraded.

INSTALLATION

First determine where you want to place the unit or units on your boat. If you are mounting a screen on a console or gunwale, it is important to make sure that nothing obstructs the tilting action of the mount, and that the screen is easily visible to the opertor. Then, using the bracket as a template, mark and drill the mounting holes after making sure you have access under the mounting area. Be sure that you are not drilling into electrical wiring or solid components. Bolt the bracket in place.

POWER CABLE

For best results the power cable should be run directly to the boat's battery. If the cable is not long enough, add a splice with #18 gauge insulated wire. The cable can be connected to a fuse buss on the console, but in some cases, this may create electrical interference. It is extremely important to have the supplied fuse wired into the power cable. The cable should be kept away from other wiring, especially the engine wires, to prevent electrical interference, a major cause of sonar problems.

To avoide damage caused by striking underwater obstacles, most transom-mounts are fitted with a kick-up bracket that allows the transducer to swivel up and out of the way if struck.

ELECTRICAL INTERFERENCE

Electrical noise usually appears on the display as a random pattern of dots or lines and, in extreme cases, can cause the unit to operate erratically or completely cover the screen with black dots. To diagnose the cause of electrical interference (with the boat in the water), turn off all electrical equipment including the engine. Switch on your sonar unit. There should be a steady bottom signal on the display. Then turn on each piece of electrical equipment on the boat, one at a time, monitoring your display screen with each addition. If you find noise interference from a particular component, you can usually reroute the sonar unit's power cable and transducer cable away from the wiring that is causing the problem.

If no electrical noise is found, shut down all electrical equipment except the sonar and start the engine. With the gearshift in neu-

tral, increase the rpm. If interference appears on the display, the problem could be one of three things: spark plugs, alternator or tachometer wiring. Try using resistor spark plugs, alternator filters and/or routing the sonar's power cables away from the engine wiring.

TRANSDUCER INSTALLATION

Proper installation of the transducer is extremely important. Follow the instructions in your owner's installation manual. If not installed correctly, any number of problems may result. To avoid interference on the display, the transducer should be placed in a location that has a smooth, constant water flow at all times. The transducer should also be installed with its face pointing straight down, if possible. If the transducer is mounted on the transom, make certain it doesn't interfere with transporting the

boat. The transducer should never be mounted closer than about a foot from the lower engine unit to avoid cavitation interference. The transducer should be mounted as deeply in the water as possible to keep the unit underwater at high speed to reduce the possibility of air-bubble interference. If possible, route the transducer cable away from other wiring on the boat. Electrical noise from engine wiring, bilge pumps, and aerators can be displayed on the sonar's screen.

The best location for transom installations is usually one foot from the centerline of your boat (outside the turning diameter of your propeller). Select the side where the rotation of the propeller is downward, usually the right side. It is also extremely important that the transducer is not located directly behind any strakes, ribs, outlets or any potential source of turbulence or cavitation. Turbulence creates aeration that will reflect your sonar beam and blind your display.

Most transom-mounting systems utilize a kick-up bracket that allows the transducer to kick up and out of the way if struck by an underwater obstacle. Make sure you follow the manufacturer's instructions for assembly and installation of the mounting bracket. In general, the bracket should be installed so the transducer face is 0 to ⅛ inch below the bottom of the boat hull.

Thru-hull installations provide excellent high-speed operation

Transducers for bow mounts are attached to the trolling motor.

and good-to-excellent depth capability. There is less possibility of damage from floating objects and the transducer can't be knocked off when docking or loading on the trailer. There are, however, some drawbacks. Some loss of sensitivity does occur, even on the best hulls. This varies from hull to hull and even among different installations. This can be caused by differences in hull lay-up and construction. Also, the angle of the transducer can't be adjusted for the best fish arches. This can be a problem on some boats that sit with the bow high in the water at rest or at slow trolling speeds.

Generally, transom-mount installations are preferred when the absolute highest sensitivity and quality of fish arches is the goal. Some sonars offer speed and temperature, as well as trip-log information, with special transducers. Speed and temperature information is not available with thru-hull installations.

Most thru-hull installations are located in the bilge area. Prior to bonding check to see that the surface of the hull is flat so that the entire transducer is in contact with the hull. Make certain that the area is clean, dry, and free of oil and grease. Lightly sand the inside surface of the hull and the face of the transducer with 100-grit sandpaper. Follow the instructions on the epoxy package, being careful to mix it evenly and thoroughly.

Apply a small amount on the face of the transducer and to the sanded surface of the hull. Place

the transducer into the epoxy on the hull, twisting it to force any tiny air bubbles out from under the transducer face. The face of the transducer should be parallel with the hull, with a minimum amount of epoxy between the hull and the transducer. Let the epoxy dry completely before use.

If you fail to get good fish arches on your display, the transducer could be out of parallel with the bottom when the boat is at rest or at slow trolling speeds. If the arch slopes up but not back down, the front of the transducer is too high and needs to be lowered. If only the back of the arch is printed, the nose of the transducer is angled too far down and needs to be raised.

BOW-MOUNT INSTALLATION

Mounting a sonar unit on the

bow, with the transducer fastened onto the boat or a part of the trolling-motor housing, provides the most detailed view from the bow fishing platform. Both the Pinpoint and certain Universal Transducer Minn Kota trolling motors have solved the problem of attaching the transducer to the trolling motor by providing built-in units. For trolling motors without these features, mounting the transducer is still fairly simple. You can use either a motor bracket available from the manufacturer or a large hose clamp. Position the transducer to aim straight down when the motor is in the water. Use plastic ties to attach the transducer cable along the trolling motor shaft. Make certain there is enough slack in the cable for the motor to turn freely. Route the cable to the sonar unit and the transducer is ready to use. Install the sonar unit in the appropriate place on the bow deck.

Chapter 6

Batteries and Chargers

It is important to keep track of battery condition and a good hand-held tester, such as the Schumacher model shown here, can indicate the charge, and whether a battery needs to be replaced.

A sinking feeling is not always a boat going down. It can be a boat that won't go. One pro said it best a couple of years ago: "A dead battery makes a $35,000 bass boat worthless." Indeed, your batteries are some of the most important pieces of equipment in your boat. The first step to prevent being dead in the water is to purchase quality batteries that match your boat and fishing needs. Two types of marine batteries are needed: a cranking battery for starting your engine and a battery (or batteries) for your trolling motor. Batteries are also used to power electronics such as GPS or sonar units, run navigation or other types of lights and for other chores such as operating electric anchors. Before you buy a marine battery, it's important to determine how you plan to use it. It's best to purchase a cranking battery for your engine and a deep-cycle marine battery for trolling motor applications. Some batteries such as the Sears DieHard and Stowaway PowerCycler are available as a combination Marine Starting and Deep Cycle for trolling motors.

BATTERY TECHNOLOGY

Marine batteries have traditionally used lead/acid technology with sulfuric acid as the electrolyte. Three different lead/acid technologies are available: wet cell, absorbent glass matt (AGM) and gel cell. Wet cells are the oldest, and use liquid electrolyte with lead plates. They have less weight per ampere-hour than AGM or gel cell batteries. Removable caps allow access to the electrolyte, and they are more tolerant of overcharging and higher charging rates. As a rule, however, wet-cell batteries don't last as long nor carry a charge as long.

Gel technology makes use of fluid electrolyte that has been processed into a nonspillable, jelly-like material. These batteries are maintenance free, and do not release gas and vapors. Gel-cell batteries are fully submersible, highly resistant to shocks and vibrations, and have low self-discharge rates.

Absorbent glass mat (AGM) batteries produce energy the same way as wet cell or gel-cell batteries. They differ, however, from wet-cell batteries in that they are valve-regulated lead/acid (VRLA) batteries. AGM batteries are fully sealed and contain a special pressure-relief valve that ensures safety and prevents air from entering. AGM batteries are packed tightly with a glass mat separator that absorbs the fluid electrolyte. AGM batteries are maintenance free,

may be installed at any angle in confined spaces, and are highly resistant to shocks and vibrations.

Nickel/zinc batteries offer an alternative. Instead of using lead and acid as the primary materials for creating a battery, they use nickel and zinc. Nickel/zinc batteries will last from five to 15 times longer than lead/acid batteries and have up to 60 percent longer run time per day than lead/acid batteries.

BATTERY NEEDS

It's important to purchase high-quality batteries that have enough capacity to operate your equipment. Lead/acid batteries are rated by amp hours. Add the amp requirements of your gear – amp requirements will be marked on trolling motors and electronic gear – then determine your approximate run time in hours. Multiply this by the amps needed for run time to determine the number of ampere-hour battery you need.

BATTERY TESTING

Use a hydrometer to check the specific gravity of the electrolytes in each cell. A fully charged battery will have a specific gravity of 1.265 to 1.280 per cell. This requires removing the vent caps and checking each cell of the battery for specific gravity levels. If the specific gravity level is low,

the battery should be recharged prior to use.

A second method of testing is the voltmeter. A fully charged battery will have a voltage reading of 12.7. If you have a gel battery, its vents cannot be opened; therefore you can't check the specific gravity and

Bass Boat Facts
Battery Requirements

Quality batteries should last for four to five years, if properly used and maintained.

- Electric trolling motor (12-volt): One 12-volt, deep-cycle battery.
- Electric trolling motor (24-volt): Two 12-volt, deep-cycle batteries rigged in series.
- Electric trolling motor (36-volt): Three 12-volt, deep-cycle batteries rigged in series.
- Outboard: Combination starting/deep-cycle battery that also supplies power to your electronics. (Many tournament anglers these days are installing a fifth battery to operate electronics and livewell.

Wiring a Pinpoint Motor

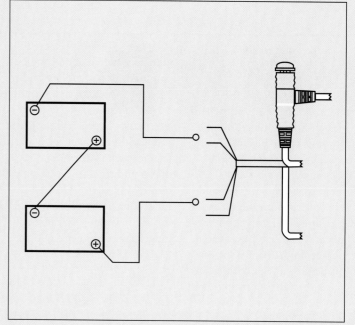

Most bass boats run 24-volt systems with two batteries wired in series for the trolling motor. Some bass boats run three batteries for a 36-volt system.

Wiring for a Pinpoint Positioning Motor – such as the diagram for the 24-volt system shown above – eliminated the need for split voltage for operation.

must use a voltmeter. Test probes with sharpened ends are touched to the battery and you read the results.

Permanently mounted battery gauges, such as the panel mounted Goldeneye II Battery Energy Gauge, tells the power remaining while on the water. The Guest Systems Voltage Scanner shows battery voltage second by second using an onboard computer and tells if your battery charger and alternator are performing properly. Cruising Equipment's BUG (Battery Use Gauge) is a combined digital voltmeter and microprocessor. The BUG is available in 12/24, 32/36 and 48V versions.

BATTERY MAINTENANCE

Quality marine batteries, both deep cycle, and starting, should last up to four or five years with good maintenance and proper use. If you're experiencing shorter battery life, several factors may be the culprit(s): low quality, improper maintenance, overheating, misuse or neglect. Misuse includes extreme deep cycling, overheating caused by overcharging, and failure to maintain proper fluid levels.

Maintenance steps:
1. Check electrolyte levels in each

cell before charging. Use deionized or distilled water to refill. Avoid overfilling.
2. Keep the batteries dry and clean. Periodic washing with a mild solution of water and baking soda is recommended, along with regular inspection for corrosion accumulations.
3. Remove corrosion with a wire brush. Scrub the terminals and use a clean rag to wipe the rest of the battery's case. Always rinse with clear water and dry the battery thoroughly.
4. Clean the battery terminals, cable connectors and all accessory connectors every month.

Onboard chargers, permanently connected to the trolling motor batteries, make it easier to charge and maintain a charge. The MotorGuide Max Pro chargers shown here automatically shut off when batteries are fully charged and turn back on when a charge is needed, preventing damage from over- or under-charging.

CHARGING BATTERIES

Using the proper charger can also make a difference in the life of your batteries. Choices include saltwater models, waterproof models for onboard use, etc. Don't select a charger that will charge up to a certain point and cut off without topping off the charge. This produces only a surface charge (70 to 75 percent) and leads to deterioration. You also don't want a charger that just keeps on going without backing down. A charger that works too fast generates too much heat and accelerates water loss, while one that trickles energy into the battery too slowly may not always restore power completely within a reasonable time. The charger should have a "float," or maintenance, feature. The float mode keeps a constant voltage on the battery instead of meeting amperage.

Charge your battery promptly to restore its power. The charging process reverses the chemical actions that take place in a battery during discharge. When restored to full charge, the battery is ready to work at peak performance. Prompt charging is important because a battery that is completely discharged, left partially discharged over a long period of time will have a shorter life span.

A deep-cycle battery, especially built to supply power to electric accessories for hours at a time, should be recharged after each day's use. A starting battery, since it should be used only for cranking purposes, needs less frequent attention, but should be checked regularly. Quick-charging works fine with a starting battery, but a deep-cycle battery cannot absorb the massive push of amps without damage and should be recharged slowly.

With a deep-cycle trolling motor battery, the best thing you can do when you come in off the water is to immediately recharge the battery. If batteries are to be stored for any length of time, they must be maintained, or kept on a charger that has maintenance features, to prevent overcharging. Always store your battery in a cool, dry place.

Chapter 7

Boat Plumbing

Livewells are an important component in modern bass boats, primarily due to the need to keep bass alive during tournaments. Most boats feature timer controlled livewell aeration.

The cover of a bass tournament magazine from the 1970s features a photo of me with a stringer of huge bass hung over my shoulder. Those days are gone thank goodness. Not the big bass, but stringers of bass at tournament weigh-ins. Years ago, tournament directors and bass boat manufacturers saw the need for a method of keeping bass healthy and alive, and the livewell became an important element in bass boat design. These days, you can place a vigorous bass inside a livewell and expect it to stay healthy and lively, even throughout a hot summer day. Livewells have come a long way from the old days when they were simply a small, square, wooden well covered with fiberglass and filled with water from a small pump.

LIVEWELLS

Many livewells are molded of ABS plastic, with rounded corners and smooth interior sur-faces. Aluminum wells are the rule in many aluminum boats. Properly constructed, they offer no sharp edges or rivets to cause injury to the fish. Modern livewells tend to be bigger, and many manufacturers provide two separate livewells. Some livewells have a full-size lid and a smaller opening for placing fish in the livewell. This makes it harder for a fish to jump out and reduces the exposure to daylight that can cause bass to jump or thrash around. As a result fewer fish die of injuries. Many livewells are located in the stern of the boat, which reduces the pounding that fish get in the bow during long rides across rough lakes.

In addition to construction and location, the system of providing water and aeration is just as important. "Livewell systems have come a long way," says Roger Miller with Flow-Rite Controls, Ltd. "The first systems used a common bilge pump mounted to the floor of the livewell, with a stand pipe to an overhead nozzle. Although this was a heck of an improvement over a stringer, the heat generated by the pump motor excessively warmed the water, thus hindering the oxygen absorption. Drain control was simply a drain plug and filling was by gravity." Later thru-hull transom-mounted pumps could provide fresh water and fill to a higher-than-lake-level overflow, but a transom-mounted pump could not circulate nor aerate while the boat was on plane. If the pump was left on while on plane, it could cause premature

Various livewell systems are available on the market. Quality boats have molded plastic livewells with rounded corners. Single livewells can be divided with an insert, but double livewells offer better opportunities to keep catches separate and less crowded.

pump burnout.

In 1985, Flow-Rite introduced their Flow-Rite Tournament Reversible Check Valve Livewell Control System. Flow-Rite's system eliminated both the need for separate transom and livewell pumps and manual livewell drain. Whenever the boat is off plane the aerator pump draws water from the livewell drain and the lake simultaneously and sprays this mixture into the livewell, keeping it full, while expelling used and excess water through the overflow. When the boat is up on plane, the control valve automatically closes the transom port to hold the water in the livewell and the pump circulates and aerates while running from one spot to another. With the boat at rest the system automatically replenishes any water lost through the overflow.

Several years ago, Flow-Rite introduced the Powerstream Aerator. Since hot water does not absorb oxygen as efficiently as cold water, it is imperative to provide cool water and the maximum amount of oxygen to all levels of the livewell, especially during the hot summer months. Most of the oxygen provided by an overhead spray head will be limited to the top few inches of water in the livewell. Much of this treated water is immediately expelled through the overflow. The Powerstream Aerator injects freshly oxygenated water directly to the lower part of a livewell tank in a spinning motion. A venturi at the top of the aerator increases the oxygen content while a mixing tube enhances absorption.

The Flow-Rite REF 3-Position Valve and Rotary Actuator System was originally designed for shallow-draft boats, such as "flats" and aluminum bass boats, and for deep-V boats with elevated livewells. It is rapidly becoming the system of choice for many high-performance fiberglass bass boat manufacturers and professional bass anglers. The system is compact, accessible, and can be operated from any area of the boat. This means the once-dreaded task of servicing an aerator pump or livewell control valve can be a comparatively easy experience. Many builders are taking advantage of this feature and locating this control system in easily accessible areas.

LIVEWELL COOLING

During the summer months, a serious problem is catching bass from deep, cool water, then introducing them into a livewell containing warm surface water. In 1991, Charger produced the first livewell cooling system. Their ProAir system circulates a constant flow of cool water through two livewells using two pumps to draw the water from the bottom of the livewells and force it through copper coil tubes located inside the insulation of an ice chest built into the boat deck. Crestliner Boats' Enviro System also circulates livewell water through an ice chest coil. The water then cycles through a variable pulsating pump bringing the water temperature down to a level that's closer to the temperature your catch is accustomed to.

LIVEWELL SYSTEMS

A basic livewell system consists of a pump, switch, hose, intake, overflow, and livewell spray head. More advanced systems may include aerators and remote open and close valves. A wide variety of livewell pumps, recirculating pumps, switches, and controls are available. Livewell pumps come with different water volume ratings ranging from 500 up to 750 gph from Mayfair, Rule, Attwood, Marine Metal Products, and T-H Marine.

Pumps can be installed in the bilge, directly through the transom, or at other locations using a separate thru-hull pick-up. But again, they must be below water level to operate. Livewell pumps are available with three types of intake tube in-line, 90 degree, and angled which provide a range of mounting choices to suit different compartment configurations. Switches vary from a simple off-on toggle to a livewell control center with both manual and fully automatic controls which use timers to automatically turn your livewell off and on. You'll need hoses to reach from the intake to the livewell and from the overflow portion of the well to the over-

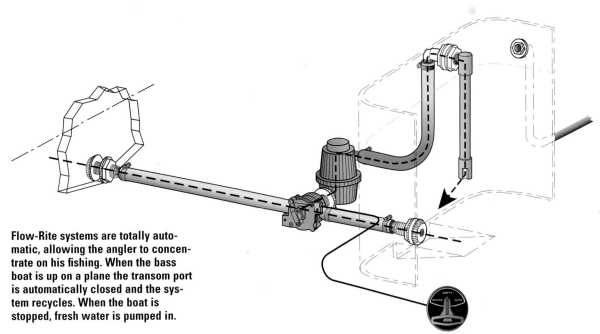

Flow-Rite systems are totally automatic, allowing the angler to concentrate on his fishing. When the bass boat is up on a plane the transom port is automatically closed and the system recycles. When the boat is stopped, fresh water is pumped in.

flow discharge fitting. You'll also need a thru-hull overflow fitting as well as a spray head assembly for adding air to the water coming into your livewell.

A simple way of installing a system is to use the Mayfair Basspirator Livewell Aerating System, a kit complete with 500-gph pump, 7 feet of ¾-inch hose, aerating head, two 1½-inch overflow fittings and hose, illuminated and fused switch, and 16 feet of 16-gauge wire, wire nuts, and full instructions.

INSTALLATION

First, determine the location of the pump. Since these pumps are not self-priming, they must be located below the at-rest water line as low on the transom as possible. Make sure you check the location and determine that there is enough room for the pump before boring any holes. The simplest method is to install the

pump through the transom. Using a hole saw, cut the appropriate-sized hole (just large enough for the threaded fitting). Place marine sealant around the pump insert face, and position the threaded intake tube in the hole. Add more marine sealant as needed and tighten the exterior lock nut over the threaded tube. You can either cut the excess tubing off with a hacksaw or, better yet, allow sufficient tubing to protrude and attach a T-H Marine Stainless Steel Wire Mesh Strainer over the outside. This prevents weeds, mud, and other debris from being sucked up by the pump.

Fasten one end of the hose to the pump discharge with a hose clamp and use another clamp to connect the other end to the livewell spray head fitting. If you're building a livewell from scratch, the spray head fitting should be placed near the top of the livewell box. In the Basspirator kit, the spray head-intake fitting is onepiece and is designed to be

A remote drain control allows you to empty the livewell without having to reach down into the tank to pull the plug. It automatically fills and drains by the turn of a switch.

installed horizontally. Marine Specialties' Flow-Rite Power-stream Aerator is installed vertically to force water and air through the bottom outlet.

The next step is to install the overflow system. This consists of a 1¼- inch outflow fitting in the upper portion of the livewell box and a 1¼-inch hose and discharge fitting through the boat hull. The

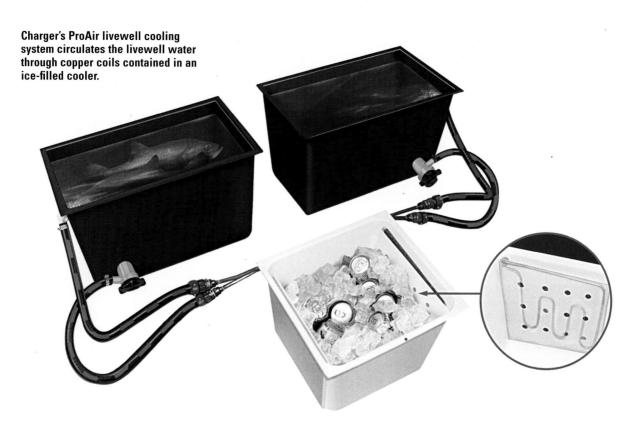

Charger's ProAir livewell cooling system circulates the livewell water through copper coils contained in an ice-filled cooler.

discharge fitting must be lower than the livewell outflow and of a larger size to assure proper drainage. The next step is the installation of the drain line. In the T-H Marine System, a removable tube fits into the bottom drain tube opening and acts as an overflow. Removing the tube allows the livewell to drain. With two livewells you will have to run tubes front and back or to either side in the rear, depending on the boat style.

You have the option of adding recirculation pumps to each livewell, which uses the water in the well, recirculating it and adding air at the same time. These are especially useful while the boat is under way, preventing the loss of fish on long boat runs. Recirculation pumps are available from several companies, including Attwood, Marine Metal Products, and T-H Marine.

BILGES

Most of us tend to ignore bilge pumps until something goes wrong. Let's face it: Pumping fresh water into your livewell and keeping it out of your boat are two very important facets of successful and safe bass fishing and tournament angling. If you have problems, you can perform many repairs yourself, and can also upgrade or add bilge pump systems. The biggest problem you'll have is running wires to the switches or pumps from the bat-tery.

BILGE PUMPS

The first consideration is the amount of water the pump will move. This ranges from around 360 up to almost 3,700 gallons per hour (gph). The most commonly used model for bass boats is a 500 gph; however, 1,000- to 1,500-gph models will provide more water removal and may be a better choice, particularly on boats used

It is easy to upgrade bilge or livewell pumps with any of the nu-merous after-market pumps and fittings.

in rougher water.

Pumps can be controlled with either manual or automatic switching. Automatic pumps come on when the bilge begins to fill, which can be a boat saver if you don't happen to notice your boat, is filling. Several years ago, an overnight driving rainstorm filled a number of boats at a dock I was using. My Charger had an automatic bilge pump and was one of the few floating normally the next morning. An automatic float switch can be added to any manual pump and a switch guard will prevent debris from jamming the auto switch in either on or off position. Three-way panel switches allow you to run the pump manually or on automatic.

INSTALLATION

Centrifugal bilge pumps are not self-priming, and must be located in the deepest part of the bilge or below the level of the water they need to pump. Any pump, however, must be accessible for cleaning and maintenance. Bilge pumps can be fastened in place with screws through the sides of hull struts in aluminum hulls and some fiberglass boats, or epoxied in place in fiberglass boats.

Make sure you use switches that are properly rated to handle your pump amperage, and be sure to install the correct size of wire so there won't be an amperage drop that allows the pump to cut its flow rate. Always install an accessible fuse in the wiring line. If you will be using an automatic switch, it's a good idea to wire the pump directly to the battery rather than through a distribution panel. This allows you to turn off the panel and leave your boat without also turning off the bilge pump.

Run the discharge hose from the pump to a through-hull fitting in the transom or the side of the boat. Do not use corrugated hose, as it will greatly reduce the flow of water. The discharge opening must be located above the water line at all angles of the keel of the boat. The longer the hose length and the higher the discharge, the more the pump has to work. The discharge opening in the hull or transom can be cut using a portable electric drill and hole saw attachment of the appropriate size. The fitting is then placed in position with marine sealant to prevent water from splashing in through the opening. Hose clamps are then used to fasten the hose to the pump and discharge fitting.

Chapter 8

Rigging Tips

Basic rigging generally begins with the installation of engines and engine controls. Make sure you follow manufacturer's instructions.

*I*n previous chapters we've discussed installing outboard engines, jackplates, mounting trolling motors and electronics. In most instances, the manufacturer or dealer does the rigging, but you may wish to do some yourself or upgrade your boat to include better equipment.

TOOLS

Many a boat has been rigged under a shade tree, and I've rigged a few that way myself. A garage, workshop or other type of shelter, however, offers a better place to store tools and shelter your work in progress. You could basically rig a boat with a few hand tools, but several power and specialty tools make the chore easier. To install heavy engines, a chain hoist or other heavy-duty lifting device is necessary. An air compressor

and a variety of air tools can also help. These include air wrenches and sanders, spray guns and dust blowers. A good shop vacuum will easily remove fiberglass fibers or metal filings.

One of the most versatile tools is a cordless electric drill. Drills are useful for boring small holes, cutting larger instrument-gauge holes, and can be fitted with different drivers. You will also need a set of wrenches, including metric sizes for some engines. The wrench set, box-open end and socket, should

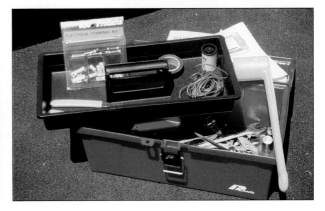

A compressor and air-powered tools along with a cordless electric drill can be useful when installing a heavy engine. A wrench set with both box-open and socket wrenches and an electrical tool kit are also handy items.

include the most popular sizes. You may also need a torque wrench. Other tools should include screwdrivers and pliers, tape measure, hammer, electrical crimping and stripping tool, solder gun, battery-load tester and charger, and a multimeter for testing electrical circuits.

One of the hardest chores is running wiring or cables through a fully assembled bass boat. A handy tool that you can easily make for yourself is a rigging-wire. This is

simply a stiff (9-gauge)wire long enough to reach through the boat. The wire has a small loop on one end and a larger loop on the opposite end. In a pinch a couple of straightened coat hangers taped together will do.

ENGINE CONTROLS

Most bass boats come from the dealer with engines and controls pre-installed and the dealer also handles most upgrades. If you do decide to perform the chore yourself, make sure you read the installation manual and thoroughly understand all phases, paying particular attention to the adjustment of throttle and shift con-

trols. It's extremely important to match the correct throttle and shift control to the appropriate engine. An important consideration is the length of the control cables. Cables that are too long result in unnecessary bends, and cables that are too short sometimes develop sharp bends with kinks.

The first step is to select a mounting area on the inside of the gunwale for the control panel. Cut an opening for the cables and drill for the appropriate bolts using the template supplied with the unit. Connect the cables to the remote control following the procedure specified in the installation manual. Run the cables through the gunwales and out of the bilge area to the engine. Mount the remote-control panel as directed in the installation manual and make the wiring connections according to the wiring diagram specified for the remote control being installed. The ignition choke/switch and horn wiring must be run and the switch/choke and horn switches installed. Before the remote control is securely fastened, verify that all parts are in place. Also be sure that the control cables and wiring harness are routed correctly. Next install and adjust the shift and throttle cables as outlined in the installation manual. Any number of "boots," or cable enclosures, are available from T-H Marine to contain the control cables where they exit from the bilge and attach to the engine. In some instances, the fuel line may also be enclosed for protection.

Several final checks must then be done. Recheck the tightness of the control handle-retaining bolt, and torque to the foot-pounds recommended in the installation manual. Recheck and secure the control module, throttle cable, and shift cable-retaining screws. Operate the control handle several times according to the di-rections in the installation manual. Any binding or stiffness is usually caused by bends or tension on control handles close to the control, or by having too many bends in the cables. Bends that are too tight in the engine linkage can cause binding. It's important to check the operation of the neutral-start switch.

STEERING

When mounting a new steering system in the console ensure that the steering wheel will not interfere with other equipment. Check for adequate space behind the dash for fitting connections. The helm should always be secured with the self-locking fasteners supplied by the manufacturer. Substituting non-self-locking fasteners can result in loosening or separation of equipment and loss of steering control.
- Hydraulic: In hydraulic systems the vent and filler plug must be installed at the top of the unit. Next, install the elbow fittings for the hydraulic system and fasten the hoses to the helm behind the console. Route the hoses through the gunwale to the bilge compartment and out to the engine location. Attach the hydraulic cylinder to the engine and connect it to the engine tiller arm. The final step with a hydraulic system is to fill with the appropriate hydraulic fluid and bleed the system to eliminate any air.
- Cable: If the unit is cable steer, run the cables as per the instruction manual and fasten to the engine tiller arm as directed.

Steering systems, such as this hydraulic system made by SeaStar, are fairly easy to install.

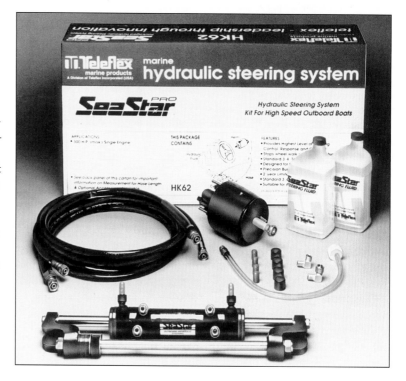

For either system, mount the steering wheel to the helm and tighten the steering wheel-shaft nut to the proper torque.

WIRING

Only marine-grade wire should be used for trolling motors and electronics. Marine-grade wire is a multi-stranded wire with a copper core. Each strand is tinned to prevent corrosion. Examine the wire after a portion has been stripped; tinned wire will have a slight silvery appearance. Stranded wires are more flexible than solid wires, making them easier to thread through tight areas. Marine-grade wire is longer lasting because it resists kinks and bends, is fire resistant, and specially insulated to prevent deterioration in a wet environment.

The wire should always be of the appropriate size. Most riggers consider 6-gauge wire to be the best for wiring bow-mount trolling motors, and 10-gauge for the primary electronics system. Smaller wires, down to 16 or 18 gauge, can be used to wire individual circuits. The appropriate fuses or circuit breakers must be installed to protect all wiring. These should be rated to the amps specified by the manufacturer for heavy-duty 24- and 36-volt trolling motor systems. Other circuits should be protected by the fuse size suggested by the manufacturer.

Pulling wires through the boat is fairly easy with a rigging-wire.

Thread the rigging wire through the wiring tunnel or other open area. Make a loop in the wire to fit through the rigging-wire loop and use plastic electrician's tape to seal off the loops and create a snag-free connection. Simply pull on the rigging-wire to draw the electrical wire through the space or tunnel and disconnect the rigging-wire.

Some of the biggest headaches with boat wiring are loose connections. Loose connections can cause everything from dead-in-the-water problems with the main engine and trolling motor to the failure of electronics and lights as well. Eliminating unnecessary connections is the first step, followed by using the proper connectors. Crimp-on connectors are the most common choice of electrical connection for most marine applications. Remember to match

the the size of the connector to the wire size. If the connector is too small, it's hard to get the strands smoothly inserted and some strands may be bent back and out. Too large and the connector doesn't contact all the strands properly. In either case the connector will rob the system of power.

Making a good connection with crimp-on connectors begins by cutting the wire to the proper length, useing a good cutting tool that leaves a clean, flat end. Strip the proper amount of insulation from the wire end, leaving just enough to fit into the connector without having excess wire exposed. Use the proper-sized crimping tool to crimp the connector down firmly onto the wire. Be sure that the crimp is secure and attached to the metal portion of the connector just overlapping the insulation.

Soldering Tips

Soldering assures a long-lasting connection. Use heat shrink tubing over the connection for more protection.

1. **Thoroughly clean the area to be soldered. A piece of 4X, or extra fine steel wool can be used to lightly buff and clean the joint. Brush on a bit of flux to further clean the area.**

2. **Plug in the soldering gun, turn it on and "tin" it as it begins to heat by touching the end of the solder roll to the gun tip.**

3. **Heat the joint thoroughly, using the entire tip surface of the gun.**

4. **Apply solder to the heated joint at the point of the gun tip contact. It will run into the connection. Don't over-solder, as you're only wasting solder.**

5. **Allow the solder to cool before moving the connection.**

6. **After use, clean the tip with steel wool and tin the tip again prior to storage.**

7. **To prevent heat moving toward delicate electronics, use a "heat sink," which is a metal object such as clamp-on pliers positioned to deflect the heat.**

SOLDER JOINTS

Soldering assures a good, solid, long-lasting electrical connection. Although you can do electrical soldering with a small propane torch, a quality electric soldering gun makes the chore easier and more precise. A dual-watt gun, such as the 400/150-watt Craftsman Professional Soldering Gun, provides even more control and ease of use. It rapidly heats the soldering tip to the proper temperature and automatically maintains heat at the tip during the soldering process.

Solder is available with two types of flux — rosin core for electrical work, and acid core for general purpose soldering. For electronics and electrical connections, use only rosin-core solder. Acid core should only be used when the flux residue can be washed away. For connections on boating electronics and trailer wiring, strip the wires back approximately three-quarters of an inch and twist them together in a pigtail splice. Make sure the splice is tight and solid and that both wire ends are equally twisted. If only one end twists and the other stays straight, it's harder to make a solid connection.

Any electrical connection must be protected from the elements and covered to prevent it from grounding out by touching other metal objects. Electrician's tape can be used, but a better alternative is a "liquid electrical tape" such as that from Star Brite. The liquid can also be applied to the terminal screws of a battery to prevent connections from vibrating loose. The liquid is simply painted on.

A piece of heat-shrink tubing will add further strength, more insulation, and better moisture protection. Tubing must be cut to fit the connection and matched to the wire size. For ring connectors, cut a piece that fits from the center of the ring up over the connector end to about one-half inch up on the wire. For butt connectors, the tubing should reach approximately one-half inch up on the wire past each end of the connector. The best method of heating is to use an electric heat gun, but a match, lighter, or mini-torch will work as well. Once the tubing has been tightly shrunk in place, use a sharp knife to trim the excess from the ring area.

INSTALLING ON-BOARD CHARGERS

On-board chargers have become so popular with bass boaters that many manufacturers offer them as either standard or optional equipment. After-market installation of on-board chargers is fairly easy. Choose a mounting location that will support the charger. In many instances, this will be on the inside of the transom. Make certain that the charging leads will reach the batteries. Position the charger over the mounting location and, using the mounting holes as a template, mark the

holes. Drill the mounting holes and secure using the screws supplied with the charger. Use silicone marine sealer to waterproof the screw holes.

On-board battery chargers come with a male-end AC power cord that can either be left loose in the bilge or fastened to a convenient location with a simple strap clamp. A better method is to use an exterior plug placed on the inside of the boat gunwale. This will allow you to plug an extension cord into the exterior plug without opening the bilge/fuel area. The plug must be hard-wired from the charger, or you can use a universal charger cord outlet.

Most on-board chargers have a monitor window for each bank of batteries to indicate the charging level. But you still must open the bilge to determine the charge level. Remote monitors provide instant information and are relatively easy to install.

INTERIOR LIGHTS

Many bass-boat manufacturers offer lots of bells and whistles such as livewell lights and locker interior lights. Courtesy lights scattered around the boat also add to the amenities. If you're a night angler, you'll find these lights not only helpful, but an added safety factor as well. If your boat doesn't offer the luxury of these lights, you can add them quite easily with aftermarket lights and lighting kits.

Fixed utility, or courtesy lights, for cockpits or other areas around the boat are available from Hellamarine, Perko, Attwood, Anderson, Aqua Signal, Boat Lighting and Equipment, and T-H Marine. T-H Marine carries several small, economical, flush-mounted courtesy lights as well as livewell lights. The courtesy lights are available with or without a protective lens and are fitted into an opening and secured by screws from the front. T-H Marine's livewell light is totally waterproof and virtually indestructible. The bulb and socket pops in from behind, and the unit mounts just like a thru-hull fitting. Courtesy and livewell lights can be turned off and on by wiring into an existing or new waterproof accessory switch on your console. Cabela's advertises special gang-switch panels and T-H Marine offers a waterproof push-button switch that can be mounted beneath locker and livewell lids. Installing lights, switches, and

Mike O'Shea uses his trim and steering systems in conjunction to ensure that his high-performance bass boat handles up to its full potential.

wiring can be either quite easy or extremely difficult, depending on the accessibility to work spaces and amount of trouble encountered in running the wiring. Examine your boat carefully to determine possible locations. Run the wiring as mentioned earlier, and then connect the wires from the light to the incoming electrical wires. Make sure the wires are not left dangling in places where they can catch on things, such as under the console or in a locker. Use screw-on plastic straps to fasten the wires neatly in place.

Connect to the switch or power source using the appropriate marine connectors.

PERFORMANCE RIGGING

Bass boats are designed to provide high performance "right out of the box." Many bass boat aficionados, however, desire to get the ultimate performance from their rigs. Any number of steps can be taken to increase engine, boat and driver performance.

ENGINE

Today's high-performance outboards are miracles of technology,

and anglers generally take for granted the speed and superior performance available in modern engines. There are ways, however, that you can get even more performance from a factory engine. According to Mike Walrath with Mercury Marine, "Getting the most from your high-performance engine requires a number of steps, and most important is putting together the right boat and right engine. First, there's the 60-miles-per-hour boat, the 70-miles-per-hour boat, and the 80-miles-per-hour boat. You can use the same engine to propel all those boats. Given those parameters, as far as performance, the boat probably has more to do with performance than the engine. So, if you're setting up for optimum performance, you need to first decide what kind of boat you want and what you expect out of it in the way of performance, with realistic goals and expectations. So now you've chosen a boat, let's say a 60-miles-per-hour boat. It's not a bullet or racing boat, but a good "60s" bass boat. Now match it with the proper engine. The first step is to max out the horsepower. If the boat is rated for a 150, put a 150 on it instead of a 135. If it's rated for 200, put a 200 instead of a 175-horsepower motor on it."

Most dealers will be more than happy to help you select the proper engine for your boat and style of running. According to Mike, "Most boat riggers have a boat/engine recipe pretty well dialed in. They know, given a particular boat and engine, how it should be rigged. They also generally know what prop to choose. There're lots of things you can do with props, and there's a lot of room you can play with engine locations."

A factory engine can be customized to improve performance and increase speed. A number of options are available. One thing you can do to get the most out of your motor is to install fiberglass reeds. These atomize the fuel more efficiently and give your motor a little more midrange "umph." In addition, an after-market, high-performance spark plug kit will intensify the spark and boost engine performance. High-performance spark plugs release all of

their energy at the point of ignition and increase the spark by a million volts. That makes your engine run faster and keeps it burning cleaner.

Yet another after-market product you can install are exhaust tuners. This involves pulling the power-head and installing a new "megaphone" that increases the exhaust discharge. This releases backpressure so you can go faster. Offset heads can also be installed. Serious "go-fasters" even mill the heads or replace the standard heads and with bigger heads. Tuning the lower unit

can also help. Such things as customized nose cones can increase speed and improve handling. Most bass boat owners will do best by having an experienced installer do the nose job.

"Of course, propping is also a key factor," states Mike Walrath. "Once you do all these things you have to re-prop, and that definitely needs to be done by someone who

A large wheel and well-designed console are important features in a high-performance bass boat.

knows what they're doing, because every prop is different. We can cup them, take the pitch out of them, or whatever is necessary. For instance, if the boater wants a hole shot, we have to prop it from a whole different respect than if he wants to run at top-end or midrange speeds. There's a prop for every situation and you simply have to use trial and error until you find the correct one. When running at high speeds, the difference in a prop that is "right on" and one that is not can mean the difference in several miles per hour."

RIGGING DETAILS STEERING

Moving at high speed requires a high-quality steering system. If the boat has a small steering wheel, it should be replaced with a larger one. Larger steering wheels offer better control with less hand movement and drivers experience less fatigue while driving for long periods of time at high speed. The next step is to make sure the steering system is top quality as well. The minimum you should select would be a dual cable manual steering system. The best bet, however, is a No-Feedback (NFB) hydraulic system such as Teleflex.

Experienced fishing professionals like top walleye pro and bass angler Jimmy Bell and bass pro Mike O"Shea cite safety and fatigue as two of the most important factors that come into play when it comes to operating high-performance bass boats. Both men agree that good quality equipment and proper use of the boat's steering and trim systems are crucial to control and handling, especially when exceeding 50 mph.

"Most high-performance bass boats are rigged with larger outboards, typically in the 175- to 250-horsepower class, which can generate a lot of torque," notes Bell. "Other elements, such as hull design, water conditions and trim positioning can increase the amount of torque. My Skeeter ZX195 bass boat with a Yamaha 200 EFI engine has a Teleflex SeaStar Pro steering system. If your boat isn't equipped with such a hydraulic system and you let go of the wheel at higher speeds, the considerable steering loads can cause you to spin out of control." O'Shea echoes Bell's sentiments when it comes to the importance of a high-performance boat's steering system. He has been a believer in Teleflex NFB hydraulic steering since the product's introduction, and currently has a SeaStar Pro system on his Nitro 8184 tournament bass boat.

Before heading out on the

Installation of quality trim controls plays an important role in determining the performance characteristics of high-speed bass boats.

water for a high-speed run, make sure your steering system has been properly installed and that it has been "bled" correctly. If you know the number of turns your system makes lock-to-lock (SeaStar Pro makes four), you can check for proper bleeding by turning the wheel all the way to the right and then all the way to the left. Count the number of wheel revolutions from hard over to hard over, and if it is more than four then it's likely that you have air in the system.

Another way to check if your hydraulic steering system has been bled properly is to grab the cavitation plate and push the motor to one side. A properly bled SeaStar Pro cylinder should have no more than ⅜-inch play.

TRIM

In addition to the type and quality of your boat's steering system, trim plays a very important part in performance. The way you adjust your trim controls the "lift" of the bow and how the boat will handle in different types of water conditions. When running at higher speeds, proper trim position is even more vital to achieving and maintaining maximum control. "Proper trim control is crucial to getting peak performance out of your boat," said Jimmy Bell. "To get your boat up and running at the right spot, watch your rpm vs. your mph. Also keep an eye on your water pressure. If your trim is

not adjusted properly and your motor is too high in the water, you'll probably start losing water pressure." Bell uses Teleflex water pressure gauges on his boat.

Pros like Bell and O'Shea know that when their boats are up on the pad, they don't have the same control that they do at slower speeds. Waves, wake, and debris in the water are all situations that may require trimming down quickly for better handling. Bell has installed a dual Pro-Trim switch on his tournament boat. He does not use a jackplate. Instead, he uses both of the turn-stalk momentary switches (attached to the steering column) to control trim functions, enabling him to make adjustments quickly with either hand in urgent situations.

Like Bell, Mike O'Shea uses his trim and steering systems in conjunction to ensure that his high-performance bass boat handles up to its full potential. "This equipment really comes into play when I'm on challenging tournament waters like the Delta near Stockton, California, with seemingly endless miles of slalom 'S' turns, blind corners, and narrow channels," said O'Shea. "In these kinds of situations, I keep in constant touch with my trim control and steering wheel so I can react and adjust quickly to the constantly changing conditions and water hazards."

Bell and O'Shea are both quick to point out the advantages of equipping a boat with Teleflex Pro-Trim switches, which allow

you to make necessary trim adjustments without taking a hand off the wheel. Teleflex Pro Trim switches, offered in single (for trim only), or dual versions (for both trim and jackplate), are similar to a car's turn signal stalk in design. Both foot- and stalk-style trim and jackplate switches are available from T-H Marine as well as switches that fasten directly to the steering wheel.

FOOT THROTTLE

Of course, it doesn't do any good to have the trim buttons on the steering wheel if you have to take your hand off the wheel to adjust engine power with a hand control. A floor-mounted, foot throttle is best for high-performance boating. It frees your hands for driving, and drives more like an automobile, with more precise throttle control. Factory installed hand throttles do not return to idle when you release them. Foot-controlled models do return to idle providing an extra safety factor. It is important that a foot control be located to suit your stature and driving style. I test drove a racing bass boat that had the foot throttle so far away I couldn't reach it without sitting on the edge of the seat. T-H Marine makes an adjustable mount so the foot pedal can be slid forward or back as desired. The foot throttle should snap back instantly to the idle position when your foot is removed.

STORAGE AND ADD-ONS

If you don't have it, you can't fish with it, and you can bet you'll need it when you can't find it. With today's increasing array of tackle, gear, and accessories, organization and storage quickly becomes a major problem for bass anglers. As with most other American outdoor sports, fishing has also become "gadgetized." Any number of products can be added to your bass boat to make it easier and more productive to fish from, and maybe even a little safer.

Built-in Storage

Fortunately bass boats tend to have more storage space than most other types of boats. This is mainly

SEAT WITH TRAY STORAGE

due to the fore and aft casting decks. Not only do these place the angler up high for easy casting, they provide handy spaces for below-deck storage. The quality and usefulness of storage varies a great deal from boat to boat.

Size

Can't get enough storage. That's what I used to think. In the old days, bass boat storage wasn't particularly efficient but these days storage box design is one of the major criteria in designing quality bass boats. One important feature is rod box size. Many boats have rod lockers long enough to hold even the longest flipping sticks. For instance, the rod lockers on Charger boats are big enough to crawl inside. In fact, Joe Doris of Charger delivered a Charger boat to the parking lot of a boat show in the wee hours of the morning. "I just crawled inside the rod locker and went to sleep," he related. "It was much more comfortable than sleeping in the truck. But thank goodness no one looked inside the rod locker that night. We would both have been surprised!"

Lure and Tackle Storage

Loose tackle boxes can be dangerous in rough water and sorting

through a number of tackle boxes for the lure you need may take up valuable fishing time. Many manufacturers are incorporating nifty ways of organizing tackle and gear into their boat designs. Charger has installed a removable tackle tray in their bow storage box for many years. They also have a combination holder for pork jar, scent bottle, and pliers molded into the gunwale and a map storage pocket under the driver's seat. Many manufacturers, such as Plano, are removing tackle boxes by replacing them with storage inserts that hold plastic utility boxes. Ranger and Procraft also offer built-in tackle storage systems. Triton's tackle storage is marketed as the Pro Active Lure System (P.A.L.S.).

A number of after-market storage organizers are also available. One option is the Coverlay Utility Box Caddy that keeps multiple utility boxes organized and easy to identify and transport. Each caddy stores up to six boxes securely in individual dividers. The boxes are secured with a nylon strap for easy carry. Coverlay's caddy is available in two sizes, large for 14 x 8¾ x 1⅞ inch utility boxes and small for 10¾ x 7 x 1⅞ inch boxes. Also available from Coverlay is Peter T's Rigmaster, designed to store Carolina Rigs. Created by bass pro

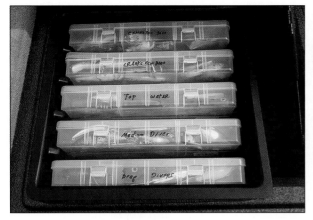

Peter Thliveros, the Rigmaster holds four leaders in place with Velcro strips and can be kept in any storage compartment.

Rod Storage
Some of the biggest changes in tackle storage are the new rod holders available for bass boats. These systems use tubes to hold the rod tips, generally with a matching tube or rack for the handles. These protect the rod tips and make it easier to store and retrieve rods. Many boat manufacturers offer rod storage as either standard or optional equipment.

After-market rod holders are available including the Coverlay Rod Box Organizer that fits in a rod box to hold 10 rods. The Quickdraw Rod Management System features aluminum rod tip tubes fastened inside the storage box. A clip bracket fastens in the rear of the rod box to secure the rod handles.

A number of portable rod holders enable you to easily remove all rods at the end of the day. These include Cabela's Angler's Tote and their Advanced Anglers Pro Rod Bags. Cabela's also has individual angler's rod covers which encase a single rod to protect it and keep it from tangling.

Keeping rods in place and handy

on the deck of the boat has also been of interest to boat designers. Most major boat manufacturers now offer partner rod ramps and straps. Front deck straps are now standard items on top-of-the-line boats. Rod Saver offers a variety of these strap holders including their Deck Mount Model that holds 4 to 6 rods. The Rod Saver Pro Stretch Model comes with one 12-inch strap for the handle end and one 6-inch strap for the tip end and holds up to 7 rods.

The Rod Buckle rod holder from Bass Pro features a fully retractable, coated web strap that extends to 24 inches. A top deck mount adapter allows you to install it without cutting holes in your boat. Rod Saver also has a handy map case with hook-and-loop back attachment that allows you to place it in a compartment or down at the side of your console.

Add-on Storage
Back when bass boats were first introduced they were pretty much open with little organized storage space. Many of us figured out how to fasten closet broom or tool holders under the gunwales to hold rods and some ingenious anglers even figured out how to add storage boxes. These days most bass boats feature enclosed storage com-

partments to more fully utilize space. Even the best bass boats, however, have some wasted space, and with a little creative organizing you can put it to good use.

The first place to look is in the bilge. Even with three batteries, a fuel tank, bilge pump, and maybe two livewell pumps, there's often some room in the bilge for storage. When I purchase engine oil in gallon cans to fill the oil tank, I also purchase a half-dozen plastic pint bottles and stuff them down

DRY STORAGE

Storing A Big Landing Net

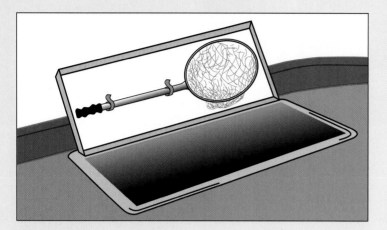

The underside of lids, including the bilge, rod locker, and other storage boxes, is another space that is often underutilized. As my bass boat is used for walleye and occasionally muskie fishing as well as for big stripers on Pomme de Terre Lake near my home, I carry a big landing net. I used to keep the net in the rod locker, but it always ended up at the bottom under a pile of rods when I really needed it. When I got a bass boat with a container in the rod locker, I finally came up with the solution of gluing hook-and-loop closure strips to fasten the net on the underside of the rod locker lid. This same arrangement can be used to store a paddle, your stern light, or other similar items. Storing maps, licenses and other papers in boats without consoles is also a problem. Heavy-duty freezer or other vinyl bags, or even a thin plastic utility box, can be held in place with hook-and-loop straps.

around the sides of the existing tank in my boat. Measure the existing space in your bilge and purchase a plastic storage box at your local hardware or discount store that will fit.

Remember your bilge will get wet. The box must be high enough not to take in water and should have a tight lid. Place a layer of foam in the bottom of the box, then add tools, or place a manufactured toolbox complete with the tools you need in the outside box. The box should be secured to keep it from shifting around and damaging the other components in the bilge.

On a fiberglass boat you can glass-in a pair of screen door handles by placing fiberglass over the ends, then use an elastic cord to secure a box in place. In some cases you may need to glass-in wooden blocks to raise the bottom of the box up off the bilge bottom. One of the best tactics is to fiberglass wooden blocks to support the box, and then use screw eyes in the top of the blocks to secure the elastic cord. On aluminum boats you may need to use screws, but make sure you are not going through the hull. Fastening through the tops of stringers is one option, but you need to use

marine caulk to fill around the holes to make sure no water can get into the stringers. Make sure you don't overfill the bilge since it need air circulation to vent fuel fumes from the enclosed space. And make doubly sure you don't block any of the vent openings.

Back in the old days when we actually sat down inside the boat instead of up on a raised casting deck, we often fastened lure holders around the inside of the gunwales. Lure holders can still be installed on today's bass boats, but their locations will depend on the boat type. You can make up your own lure holders quite easily from a piece of plastic packing foam and a strip of do-it-yourself aluminum angle stock. Glue the plastic foam to the aluminum strip, leaving about an inch of aluminum strip exposed. Bore a hole through each end of the aluminum and fasten the holder in place with sheet metal screws. Or you can simply glue a foam block in any convenient location where the lures won't be a danger or become entangled in other gear. Use a clear, flexible, adhesive such as craft glue. All you have to do is stick the hooks in the foam to hold the lures.

If you use pork or fish scents, you can provide a holder for the bottles in the front of your boat. Hook and loop closure in the form of a strap can be glued to the inside of your boat gunwale near the bow. You can also use nylon strapping fastened through the inside of the gunwale with sheet metal screws to create loops for the jars.

The space under the console

offers some additional storage space in many boats. Those with dual consoles offer even more. This is a good place to anchor a fire extinguisher, fasten a throw cushion with hook and loop closures, or even add a cup holder. A small plastic box to hold maps, your wallet, and other items and even a small first-aid kit can be installed on the side or rear of the console. The box can be held in place with hook and loop closure, or create an elastic cord strap system by glassing-in or screwing in small handles to hold the cords.

BOATER'S TOOLBOX

I always carry a boater's toolbox, regardless of whether I'm in my big bass boat or little puddle hopper — my small lake boat. First, several years ago a couple of friends and I were bass fishing up a major tributary feeding Truman Reservoir in central Missouri. As we started to leave for the afternoon my friend's old motor quit. A simple problem, a wire had burnt through. We had no wire, no tools, but with the eventual help of another angler we reached the ramp and a phone way after dark, four hours after my friend was supposed to be home for a sit-down dinner. I survived, he didn't. The second incident happened years ago while fishing for musky on Pomme de Terre, in late November. A friend and I had the lake to ourselves when a sudden storm blew in. Racing before the

wind and waves my motor gave out. We swamped fifty yards or so from a small island and ended up spending a very wet, cold night ashore. The next morning we were able to remove the motor plug, replace it with a new one, and restart the motor.

BOAT SURVIVAL KIT

A basic boater's toolbox can help you survive a break down, or at least get you home in time for dinner. First, you need something to hold your boat survival kit, and Plano makes an excellent line of toolboxes that are just perfect for the job. The toolbox should include a set of open-end wrenches and socket set for all the nuts and bolts on your boat and trailer. You should include small and large Phillips and slot-head screwdrivers. A medium-sized ball-peen hammer may also come in handy. You'll need a pair of linesman's pliers with side-cutters as well as a pair of needle-nose and electrical stripping pliers.

A prop wrench, such as the molded nylon T-H Marine Prop Master wrench, is necessary. You'll also need a block of wood to hold the prop, and I use my block as a holder for two different colors of spare electrical wire as well. An Electrical Connector Kit from S & J Products holds all the equipment you'll need to redo electrical connections. You should also carry a roll of electrician's tape. Your kit should also have spare fuses, held

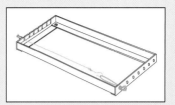
in a film canister, spare spark plugs, extra prop nut and thrust washer, spare trolling motor prop and nut. Some pros keep a spare prop. Denny Brauer keeps a spare trolling motor bolted inside of one of his rod lockers.

If you have room in your "boater's survival kit" you might also add a vial of waterproof matches and a flare kit such as the Skyblazer Marine Signal Pack. Add a few "Handi-Wipes" for cleaning grease from your hands and a soft handtowel. It can be used for drying your hands and to keep everything from rattling. Close the lid and stow your toolbox. Then hope you'll never need to use it!

Chapter 9

Boat Maintenance

Periodically the entire rig should be thoroughly cleaned to remove grime, road oil, and salt. The boat finish should be carefully inspected to determine if it needs repair.

"Landed about 45 feet up on the bank," said my friend. "First fishing trip of the season and I was so anxious to get on the water, I gassed up, charged the batteries and took off. We found the nut on the steering rod had come loose and as I made a sharp turn in the river it simply came off. We were lucky."

Boats require regular maintenance in order to work properly and safely. This should begin with a thorough preseason checkup and problems fixed before the season begins. This should be followed by regular inspections throughout the season. If the boat isn't to be used during the winter it should be winterized.

PRESEASON INSPECTION

A little preseason TLC on your bass rig before you begin the serious fishing season can prevent the possibility of an accident such as my friend had, and also protect your investment. Hopefully you winterized your rig last fall. In that case you'll have less to do. Many of us, however, simply quit fishing to enjoy other outdoor activities when winter rolls around and, if the weather is mild, also continue fishing. If you're one of the procrastinators, there will be lots more to do. Following are general preseason maintenance suggestions.

Cleaning and Inspecting

A thorough cleaning of your boat, trailer, trolling motor and engine is one of the best ways to thoroughly inspect your boat. If you've consistently kept your boat covered and clean, a one-step fiberglass cleaner/polisher can be used. Simply spray it on, then wipe it off with a soft cloth. In most in-stances, however, a thorough washing and cleaning will be re-quired. Make sure all fittings on the boat — railings, bilge breather vents and cleats — are well secured. Any found with enlarged holes in the fiberglass can be repaired with West System Epoxy Repair Pack.

Electronics and Plumbing

Check all electronics, inspect the wires and check the fuses to make sure all are in good working order. Replace any frayed or damaged wires. Inspect the bilge and livewell plumbing hoses and make sure they are secure. Several years ago, I had a boat flood on my first trip of the season because a livewell hose had come loose. Check to be sure that the drain plug is in place and fits tightly.

Trolling Motor

Modern-day trolling motors require little maintenance, but it's a good idea to check and retight-

en any loose mounting bolts or screws. Pull off the prop and check for any fouling such as fishing line, lightly grease the shaft and reinstall the prop. If the prop is damaged, now is the time to replace it. Check all bracket bolts, springs and fittings and lightly oil those that are dry. The steering cables in remote-control models are factory lubricated and adjusted to maintain firm cable tension in the foot pedal assembly. If readjustment is necessary, cable nuts

After repairs a marine wax or polish can then be applied.

Proper maintenance is not only necessary for longevity of your bass boat, motor, trailer and accessories, but also a major safety factor. Before the season begins and regularly throughout the season, thoroughly inspect the entire rig, and repair as necessary.

turned in a clockwise direction will increase the cable tension.

Outboard Engine

Check all mounting-bracket bolts and engine bolts. Make sure they are all tight. Inspect the steering system and make sure all bolts, fittings and cables or hydraulics are in good working order.

Check the level of lubricant in the lower unit and make sure it's filled to the proper level. If it looks like you have a leak, have a service expert check it out, since it could indicate that the lower seals and gaskets need replacing. And, if it wasn't done before off-season storage, drain the gear-case and refill with the manufacturer's recommended lubricant.

If your motor has a power trim or tilt unit, check the level of fluid in the system's reservoir, and refill with the manufacturer's recommended fluid as needed. If you have an engine with an oil injection system, check the engine oil level, both in the bilge and the reservoir in the engine. Make sure the main reservoir in the bilge is filled to the fill line with the appropriate engine oil. Also check your owner's manual for any special maintenance the oil-injection system might require.

Check the spark plugs. Your outboard won't start quickly and run efficiently if the plugs aren't sparking. Remove the plugs, clean them, and make sure they are gapped to specification. Also make sure the spark-plug terminal connections and wiring are clean, un-frayed and snug fitting.

If unused fuel was left in the tank and engine over the winter, it should be treated with a fuel conditioner. If no fuel conditioner was added before storage, the fuel pump filter should be cleaned before adding fresh fuel. Check the fuel line fittings and look for cracked, worn or aged fuel lines, and replace as necessary.

Consult the lubrication section of your owner's manual. Most motors require a shot of lubricant on the throttle linkage or other moving parts on the engine. On motors with remote steering, the steering cable ram should be greased before the start of each season and periodically thereafter. Once again, check the owner's manual for detailed instructions.

Check your propeller. A little ding in the prop can make a big dent in your boat's performance. If the propeller is nicked, gouged or bent, take it to the dealer or a prop shop for repair. If it's too far gone, invest in a new prop. Before

Oxidation of the gelcoat is a common problem that can be fixed with gelcoat restoration kits and materials.

removing your propeller, shift the motor into neutral and remove the key from the ignition switch to prevent the motor from accidentally starting. Wedge a piece of 2 x 4 between the prop blade and the anti-ventilation plate to keep the prop from turning. Before replacing the propeller, lubricate the prop shaft with grease as specified in your owner's manual. Also check around the base of the prop shaft for fouling by monofilament fishing line. Look closely; old monofilament might look like a plastic washer. Be sure to check your owner's manual for any special instructions and torque specifications before reinstalling the prop.

Last, but not least, fasten a water hose-connected water pump bonnet over the lower unit water intakes and fire up the engine to make sure it starts and runs properly. I always do this before the first trip of the season.

Trailer

Check the pressure in the tires, including the spare. Underinflated tires cause more blowouts on the road than anything else. Check the bearing protectors and add new marine grease if necessary. The spring-loaded piston should be approximately ⅛ inch from its seated position. Replace and repack bearings if needed. Check and tighten all lug nuts.

Make sure all lights are working. Inspect safety chains. Lubricate the tongue lift mechanism. Be sure the winch strap is connected to the bow eye of the

boat and that the winch mechanism is in the "on" position. Check the brakes and braking system if your trailer has them. Check all bolts and fasteners on the trailer winch bunk holders. Inspect tie downs and motor holder.

BOAT CLEANING

Where I live in Missouri, fishing really doesn't stop for the winter. There's still bass fishing on the Missouri/Arkansas border lakes and rivers near my home. Sometime around mid-February, I usually look closely at my boat and discover it's cleanup time.

Hull

Removing dried algae and scum from boat hulls and a lower engine unit usually calls for some elbow grease. Any number of marine-designed cleaners, polishes, waxes and other care products are available. They'll do a better job with less effort and will be better for your boat finish in the long run. Never use an abrasive cleaner on fiberglass. If using any product

not made especially for fiberglass boats, always read the label carefully. Baking soda is an excellent nonabrasive cleaner. Simply dip a damp cloth in baking soda and scrub away.

You can also take your boat to a car wash, but the soap used in these usually still leaves some scum. A better method is with a DIY car wash or pressure sprayer. These can be used with the degreasers to effectively remove scum, even in the hard-to-reach areas. A quality pressure washer can make the chore easier and quicker.

Hardware and Wood

Many of the marine cleaners, polishes and waxes can also be used on boat fittings, metal and wood, but special metal cleaners are excellent for polishing fittings. Although many products are labeled "cleaners," all manufacturers suggest washing the boat first to remove dirt and grit.

Buffing

While polishes and waxes can be buffed by hand, 3M suggests using an electric drill equipped with their 6-inch 3M Marine Superbuff

Shampoo the upholstery and clean it thoroughly. Any number of upholstery cleaners are available.

Pad and Marine Fiberglass Cleaner and Wax. The fastest and easiest method is to use a power buffer such as the Craftsman Heavy-Duty/Polisher. The best tactic with a power buffer is to apply the wax or polish with a terry cloth bonnet, and use a lamb's wool bonnet for the final buffing.

Carpeting

Even if your boat carpet looks like the back entrance to a cattle barn, it can usually be redeemed. The first step is to vacuum the carpet to remove the loose materials. If you don't have a heavy-duty shop vacuum, a car-wash vacuum will do. Some car washes even offer wet/use carpet vacuums or you might consider renting a carpet cleaner from your local rental place. Really ground-in dirt is easily removed with this method.

Stains, however, are a bit more difficult. A number of household cleaners can be used to remove even the most difficult, including fish blood and slime. These include any number of products on your grocer's shelves as well as such household items as cornstarch, baking soda, salt, club soda and ammonia. The dry powders tend to soak up immediate spills, while the club soda can be rubbed into a spot. All cleaning and stain-removing products (commercial or home) should first be tested on an inconspicuous spot such as under the console.

Upholstery

Marine upholstery and tops, including vinyl and canvas, should be cleaned and given a protective coating as well. Remember to test household and commercial products in an inconspicuous spot, and always use clean, white toweling or rags. Don't forget to rinse with clear water.

Seymour Vinyl Paint can be used to give older vinyl a newer look. Used for years in car interiors, the paint contains UV-stable pigments that guard against fading and keep that like-new look for years. The paint offers excellent adhesion to vinyl and leather. When used with Seymour Adhesion Promoter, the paint adheres to the plastic consoles found on many boats. The paint can also be sprayed on carpeting. When the paint dries, simply brush the carpet with a stiff brush to restore the carpet's original texture.

Boat Plumbing

A friend of mine — and he wouldn't wish the problem on anyone — forgot to retrieve a bass from his livewell, and left his boat in the marina slip for two weeks. When he returned he discovered not only bass soup but unhappy neighbors in the marina as well. In addition to battling the smell and mess to clean out his livewell, some of the parts and particles ended up clogging his livewell drain which required extensive repairs. That, however, is a worst-case scenario. Let's look at a more normal situation and what you can do to keep the innards of your boat clean.

Livewells

First, make sure you don't leave fish in the livewell, and drain it after each trip. Not only does this help keep it from becoming stinky, it also prevents the buildup of mildew and other bacteria that could eventually cause problems with fish held in the livewell. Many livewells do not drain completely. The residue, which usually includes fish slime, scales, and other debris, settles around the drain opening and can become odorous in a very short time. I keep a sponge to soak up leftover water and leave the livewell lids open to dry thoroughly. If the boat is to be in storage for some time, I simply place an open box of baking soda in each livewell to keep it from collecting odors.

Occasionally, however, the livewells will require a good cleaning to remove stains and odors. Chemicals added to the water to help keep your catch alive and healthy during long tournament days can cause some of the worst stain problems. Livewells can be cleaned with Bait Well/Fish Box Cleaner from Isso Products. To use the cleaner, mix a capful of the nontoxic, biodegradable powder with 2 gallons of water, and sponge it onto the livewell surface, making sure you get up under the edge of the top where mildew and mold quickly collect in hot weather. You can run the livewell pump to circulate the cleaner throughout the entire system. After soaking for 10 to 15 minutes, the surface can be rinsed down. You can also use a spray or wipe-on cleaner like Star Brite Fish Box & Bait Well Cleaner/Deodorizer.

Livewells can get pretty "stinky" and should be cleaned and freshened, not only for your own pleasure, but to provide a healthier place for holding bass.

Coolers

Many boats these days incorporate built-in coolers, and keeping them clean and mildew free is also important. At the end of each trip, make sure to open the drain and remove any debris such as sandwich bags, empty pop cans, etc. Wipe clean with a soft cloth. Place an opened box of baking soda in the cooler for extended storage.

Bilge:

Since the bilge is the lowest part of the boat, everything eventually collects there. This includes stagnant, dirty water with grime, grease and oil sludge. When you finally decide to clean the bilge, you're faced with a messy and often very difficult task, because the grime doesn't come off easily, and in most instances access to the entire bilge is extremely limited. A number of commercial cleaners are available.

REPAIRING FIBERGLASS BOATS

Fiberglass boats tend to oxidize through usage, exposure to sunlight and age. They also become scratched and gouged through use. You can do some of these repairs yourself, especially if the problems are minor. Repair of major gouges, defects, and structural damage should be done by professionals.

Gelcoat Repairs

The first step is to thoroughly clean your boat so you can detect the problems. Minor scratches and swirls can be removed with Meguiar's ScratchX scratch

Winterizing

Winterizing your boat is important. Just because your rig sits idle during the winter doesn't mean nothing happens to it. Moisture can collect in a boat, fuel can oxidize in a motor and ungreased trailer wheel bearings are subject to rust. All this is easily prevented with just a little effort.

BOAT

1. Wash and wax your boat and clean interior and upholstery. Boaters should not use a heavy-duty type of marine cleaner to clean the boat without following up with a waxing. A strong cleaner will strip off all old wax and protective sealants, exposing the gelcoat.
2. Drain water from hull and livewell lines, and lubricate the valves. Leave the bilge plug out, to avoid rainwater buildup.
3. Make sure batteries have a full charge, and store with fish finders and other electric gear in a dry area.
4. Check all electrical wiring. Replace wires that are damaged.

OUTBOARD MOTOR

1. Fill the fuel tank (if applicable) and add a fuel conditioner/stabilizer. It prevents fuel oxidation, gum and varnish deposits and inhibits corrosion in the carburetor and fuel system for up to one year.
2. Coat internal engine parts with engine-fogging oil. It helps prevent rust from moisture and acidic combustion residue in two-cycle engines during extended storage.
3. Apply a silicone protectant and lubricant to the entire engine, under the cowl and to protect other metal, rubber and plastic parts from rust and corrosion.
4. Apply a good wax to the engine exterior, to clean and protect it.

TRAILER

1. Check wheel bearings and seals for wear or rust, and repack them.
2. Touch up rusted areas on trailer. Examine trailer wiring for loose connections. Clean and lubricate all bulb receptacles.
3. Lubricate winch, and replace strap if needed.
4. Check tires for wear and, if necessary, have them balanced. If possible, block or jack up trailer to remove weight from tires during storage.
5. Repaint any paint nicks, to prevent rusting.

remover or marine rubbing compounds, such as 3M Marine's High Gloss Gelcoat Compound. The product can be applied with a 3M Marine Superbuff Pad or Hookit Compounding Pad on a slow-speed polisher turning at 1,500 to 2,500 rpm.

"Some scratches, gouges and chips can be repaired by the do-it-yourselfer," suggests Mike Shelton, service department manager of Ranger Boats. "If the damage is nothing more than a slight scratch, you can often simply sand and buff it out. Wet-sand it with 600- or 1200-grit wet-or-dry sandpaper, then hit with a heavy buffing compound, and it should shine up just like new again."

A deeper scratch or gouge requires filling with gelcoat or color putty. Mask around the area to be repaired with 2-inch masking tape, leaving an area slightly larger than the actual flaw. Sand the entire area inside the tape with #220-grit dry sandpaper, to rough up the surface and remove the shine. Wipe

off the surface with acetone and allow it to dry. Mix the gelcoat and hardener as per the instructions. With a putty knife, trowel the catalyzed gelcoat into the flaw, filling it slightly higher than the original surface, to allow for shrinkage. When the patch has cured, remove the tape and carefully wet-sand with #600-grit sandpaper to the original shape.

Repairing a small surface area of polyflake is more difficult than solid color repair because you can't sand the polyflake, as it will turn silver. To repair minor chips and scratches use the point of a knife, ice pick, or other sharp object, to scrape the inside of the flaw to ensure a good bond. Be careful not to scratch the surface around the flaw. Mix up the desired amount of touch-up polyflake premix. Using a small piece of wood or a knife blade, dab polyflake into the flaw, leaving the repaired spot slightly higher than the surrounding surface, to allow for shrinkage. Remember, you cannot sand

polyflake; the finished repair will look as you leave it. "With a polyflake scratch, you first have to fill it up with black gelcoat to back it up," said Mike. "Then you apply the polyflake with clear gelcoat. Then you need to put about three coats of clear gelcoat over that and buff it in the same way."

According to Mike, most of the materials needed for minor repairs to match a specific model Ranger can be ordered directly from the parts department. Just give them the boat's serial number and colors you need and they'll mail the materials. Many other boat manufacturers offer the same service. You can't, however, get the gelcoat hardener mailed to you. It is an illegal substance to ship, so you must get it locally. It's actually fiberglass resin hardener. Fiberglass shops, auto parts stores, hardware stores that handle fiberglass repair

kits for bathtubs, all handle the hardener. "If you have a small chip in your finish and you can't get the gelcoat hardener and stuff to fix it, we recommend a little bit of clear fingernail polish," added Mike. "Just dab a little bit of it in the chip to fill it out."

ALUMINUM BOAT FIRST AID

Preventive maintenance can protect your investment and stop minor problems before they become serious. Periodically inspect the hull for leaky rivets, dents or discolorations in the finish.

Aluminum Cleaners

Aluminum cleaners are available, including Nautical Ease Aluminum Cleaner from Nautical Technolgies. It is sprayed on, allowed to stand for 30 seconds, then rinsed thoroughly to remove discoloration, grime, scum lines and algae from aluminum surfaces. Iosso Pontoon & Aluminum Cleaner & Restorer is a paste. The surface is wetted, the paste applied, then buffed.

Aluminum Maintenance

Remove any oil or grease with an oil-free solvent. Acid brighteners can be used to remove most stains on bare aluminum. Then clean residue from the hull, using a mild detergent solution. Coat the hull with a good coat of marine wax or polish suitable for aluminum. You can use 3M Marine Trades One Step Aluminum Restorer and Polish. Simply apply a small amount of the paste with a soft cloth and rub to clean and restore the aluminum surface.

When bare aluminum can't be frequently cleaned, spray a non-yellowing protective lacquer onto a cleaned surface. If wax has been applied, wipe down with a lacquer thinner. Periodically, before the lacquer begins to wear, it should be stripped and re-lacquered.

Painted Finish Maintenance

There are several types of painted surfaces. The most common of these are enamel, polyurethane, and lacquer-based paints. Polyurethane is the most popular due to its ability to resist blistering and marring. Repairs to a

scratched surface on all of these finishes are identical. Sand with a fine-grit wet-or-dry sandpaper, and touch up with a color-matched paint from the manufacturer or dealer. Remember to allow touch-up paint to cure for at least 30 days before applying wax.

To refinish a painted boat, remove chipped, loose or blistered paint with a hand sander, using coarse-grade wet-or-dry sandpaper to remove all of the old paint. Then remove sanding scratches by sanding the entire area with medium-grade wet-or-dry sandpaper. Followed by fine-grade wet-or-dry sandpaper. If the existing paint is in relatively good condition, use only the fine-grade wet-or-dry sandpaper to scuff the surface. A rubber hand-held sandpaper block is the best choice for holding the sandpaper, as it will bend to fit the contours of the hull.

After sanding, wipe the entire hull with a cloth saturated with paint thinner, to remove dirt and sanding dust. Follow your marine supplier's recommendations in selecting flat or semi-gloss marine enamel for painting the hull. Use anti-fouling type paint below the water line in regions where it's necessary. If applying more than one coat, hand sand between coats with very fine-grade wet-or-dry sandpaper.

Clear Coated Aluminum Surfaces

A clear lacquer finish can be removed with lacquer thinner and treated the same as a bare alu-

Loose rivets on aluminum boats can be tightened by peening the inside of the rivet to expand the metal.

minum. A clear anodized finish produces a hard, glasslike protective aluminum oxide that is highly resistant to weather and oxidation. This type of finish is often used on deck hardware, window frames, and bow rails. Acid brighteners should not be used on anodized surfaces. The best maintenance for anodized aluminum is washing with detergent and waxing with a nonabrasive paste wax. If the surface is pitted with a light buildup of white aluminum oxide, a careful application of an abrasive polish may restore the sheen. If this doesn't work, light pressure with very fine steel wool and polish or wax may remove the buildup.

ALUMINUM BOAT HULL REPAIRS

Not all aluminum boat problems involve the finish. Aluminum boats get dented or punctured and rivets work loose. Minor problems can usually be repaired without a lot of expensive tools. For deep dents and large tears, however, and in cases where re-welding of structural parts is called for, you may want to have the work done at a factory-authorized marine repair shop with aluminum repair experience.

Dents
If you're handy and willing, you can pound out minor dents with a rubber mallet, using a rigid back-up block such as a large metal hammer head or a large block of wood held against the opposite

side of the dent. Begin tapping with the rubber mallet around the perimeter of the dent. Work in a circular pattern toward the center until you work out the dent.

Punctures
You can use a riveted aluminum patch to repair small to medium punctures. First, re-level the surface around the puncture by peening in the same manner as described for dents. Coat the patch with a good grade marine sealant, position in place on the outside of the hull, and temporarily anchor it with bolts and nuts at the four corners. Use rivets to install the patch permanently, removing the bolts and using rivets in the bolt-holes. You can also use a body filler to fill in irregularities in the aluminum surface. Or you can make an emergency or even permanent repair to a puncture with Star Bright Emergency Repair Epoxy/Aluminum Putty Stick. Just hand-knead for one minute and apply to the damaged area. It can be sanded, painted, drilled, tapped, and filed. This is an excellent product for

repairing those hard-to-get-to spots such as holes or cracks in joints.

Loose Rivets
Loose rivets can cause leaks and structural damage. Locate leaky rivets by putting your boat on a trailer, filling the boat with water and looking on the outside of the hull for water beads. To tighten loose rivets, hold a steel block or large hammerhead on the outside of the rivet and peen the inside of the rivet, causing the rivet to expand slightly. If new rivets are needed, solid aluminum rivets are recommended. Position the new rivet in place and peen it over as with the loose rivets. Closed-end, aircraft-type "pop-rivets" can be used to fasten aluminum boat pieces back together or replace the hull rivets. These types of rivets are necessary in some closed areas where you can't reach the back-side of the rivet. Where retightening is not possible, a sealant such as 3M 101 Marine Sealant can be used to "caulk" around minor problems. Major problems will require professional help.

Chapter 10

Trailers

A quality trailer that is matched to the bass boat is extremely important. Some boats come with more economical trailers, but the trailer can be upgraded.

Most boats spend most of their life on a trailer rather than in the water. In fact some folks seem to spend more time trailering their boats than fishing. Choosing the correct trailer is important for the longevity of your boat, as well as your safety in traveling. It also determines the ease of loading, unloading, and storing your boat.

Granted, many manufacturers today offer the boat and a matching trailer as a package deal, which may come with all the bells and whistles or just the bare bones. Usually a dealer's package trailer is one of the more economical models, chosen to make the overall price more attractive. These economy trailers are often made of ungalvanized, or painted metal, and are of simple channel construction. It may be worthwhile upgrading to a better quality trailer. While small boats don't require as heavy or elaborate a trailer, big boats require more of both. If you are purchasing a trailer separate from the boat, first look at the load capacity to make sure it will hold your boat. Then add the weight of the trailer to your tow package. You don't want to exceed your towing vehicle capability.

Trailer construction and finish is also important. Tubular steel frames are the strongest and also enclose and protect wiring. They are also more aesthetically appealing. Quality trailers are constructed with galvanized metal with a baked-on, electrostatic or powder-coating finish for a more consistent appearance.

WHEELS, PADS, AND ROLLERS

Flat, carpeted bunks are generally used on bass boat, small utility, and Johnboat style trailers. These are often called "drive-on" trailers because that's the most common method of launching and loading the boat. Roller type trailers are used on larger, multi-species, salt-water and cruiser style boats. "Roller trailers are more popular in the Northern states and the Northeast, areas where they have shallow landings," said Don Rusch, Marketing Manager for

Midwest Industries, manufacturers of ShoreLand'r trailers. "The advantage of a roller trailer is you don't have to back in the water very far to launch or load. You can back in far enough to get the engine going and basically power off or push the boat off and it will roll right in the water. Loading is the same. Some areas don't allow power-on launching or loading because of the prop wash and you must float and winch the boat on and off. A roller trailer is a lot easier than trying to winch up on a bunk."

Self-centering loading pads or

rollers help line the boat up and guide it onto the trailer, even under less than ideal conditions. It's important the rollers or bunks properly fit the boat hull not only for easy launching, but also for secure transportation and support of the boat while trailering or storing.

Most package trailers, including the more economical ones, are

Trailers are available with single or dual axles. Boat size, weight, and tow vehicle will influence the choice.

Transom savers, positioned between the engine lower unit and trailer, protect both the motor and transom.

matched to fit the hull of the boat they are mated with. How well it fits, how much support and how easy the trailer allows for loading and unloading, can vary a great deal. Some manufacturers place bunks or rollers down low, between the wheels, while others place them up on top of the frame. Lower bunks make it easier to get into the boat from the ground. Many quality trailers offer "running boards" or steps that allow you to reach into the boat without climbing up into it. In addition to the support bunks, side guide bunks can aid in loading a boat in strong current or windy conditions. Some manufacturers

offer guides as standard equipment, others as an option. After-market bolt-on side guides are available for many trailers.

Dual-axle trailers make towing of larger boats safer – not only in handling, but also in case of a tire failure. They are, however, harder to maneuver while parked. You can't wheel them around easily. Dual-axle trailers are quite a bit more expensive, and can add to the tow weight. Tire size and quality are major considerations. The larger the tire, the cooler it runs. Small tires, even on small trailers, are a common reason for flats and bearing failures.

Among the most popular options, particularly on longer trailers, is a swing-away or removable tongue. This allows a long boat and trailer combination to fit

in a smaller space. Removable tongues can also deter thieves, but are a bit more awkward to handle. Swing-away tongues don't have to be removed and are easier to work. Both tongues, however, position the lift wheel farther back on the trailer. This means you can't operate the lift crank and work the hitch receiver at the same time.

Cheap trailer lights can be frustrating. Quality trailers feature an enclosed, plug-in wiring system rather than clip together splices. This provides a more positive ground and fewer problems. The lights should also be waterproof. The amount and type of lights also varies. Simple trailers may only have tail, back and turn signal lights. Higher-grade trailers use side and rear road lights.

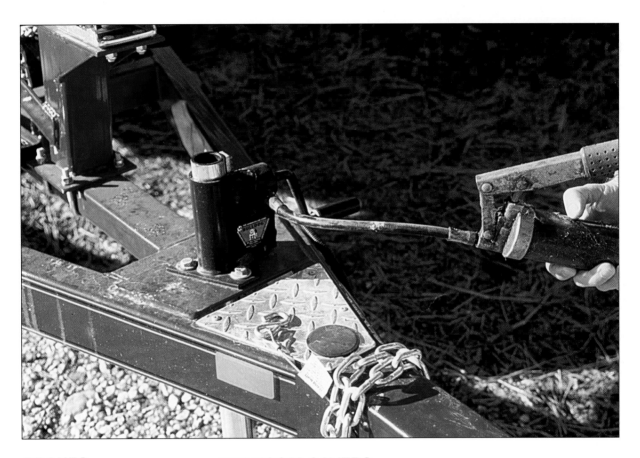

BRAKES

Most states require brakes on 3,000-pound GVWR trailers, although no national standard exists. Typically it has been the dealer's responsibility to install brakes in states that require them. ShoreLand'r has installed trailer brakes on all of their trailers rated for 2,800+ GVWR from the model year 2000. "Many consumers don't realize how difficult it can be to stop their boat and trailer package and tow vehicle in an emergency stop without trailer brakes," said Rusch.

TRANSOM SAVERS

Lift up your engine, drop the "travel lock" in place, then head down the road. You're doing fine until you forget to slow down for that railroad track and you look back in your rear view mirror to see your engine flopping up and down like a novice bull rider in a rodeo. Damage? You bet! Not only to your engine but the transom as well. Transom savers, those funny looking "props" that extend from your trailer to support the engine in an upright position, can save you a lot of money and trouble.

Travel sticks come in a variety of sizes and types, including simple, inexpensive, non-adjustable yoke sticks and adjustable yoke models that fit a wide range of configurations. Adjustable-head, spring-loaded models are also available. Some models fit over a starter roller on the rear of the boat trailer, while others fit a bracket bolted to the trailer.

Regardless of which transom saver you choose, be sure that the shock cord fits properly around the lower unit and snugs down securely. Tighten the spring-loaded Swivel-Eze unit by about ½ inch,

Trailer Maintenance

Coupler:
This is the most important connection in your rig. Check for broken washers, cracks in welded seams, twisted parts, and reamed holes. The coupler should fit firmly on the hitch ball, but not so tight that it seizes when you turn the tow vehicle. Clean the ball clamp, lubricate it with oil, and adjust if necessary.

Winch and Winch Stand:
Tighten all nuts and bolts. Unravel your winch rope or cable. If it's frayed, get a new one. Inspect the knot that connects the winch rope to the snap hook.

Trailer Jack:
Inspect the trailer jack and make sure all bolts are secure. If it has grease fitting, lightly grease it.

Frame:
Inspect for loose or missing bolts or fasteners. Tighten all the frame nuts and bolts. Shake the trailer here and there to test for soundness. Rust is a nemesis that eventually attacks all frames and fenders. Minor rusting can be removed by commercial rust cleaners or steel wool, and the patch sealed with several coats of rust-resistant paint. Major rusting may require sandblasting and complete repainting.

Tongue Weight:
Inspect for proper tongue weight. Balancing the trailer load ensures a safe, smooth ride. Tongue weight for most small-boat trailers should be five to ten percent of the loaded weight. Check the tongue weight with a bathroom scale, placing a block of wood on the scale to help distribute the weight. Use a box, crate, or chair to keep the scale at the hitching ball's height.

Tires:
Check the tire pressure. Keep your tires filled to the capacity listed on the tire. Low pressure when towing causes tires to heat up and creates wear. Check each tire when cold, then compare to the manufacturer's recommendations. Check the tread for uneven wear and rotate if necessary. Don't forget to check the spare tire capacity.

Rollers and Bunks:
If your boat has rollers, remove the boat from the trailer and spin each roller and roller arm. They should move freely. If they don't, smear them with waterproof grease. Replace worn rollers. Check the bunks for carpet wear, holes, and tears. Replace the carpet on worn bunks and reseat any loose areas with heavy-duty staples. If your trailer has adjustable bunks, tighten the nuts and bolts that hold the bunks in place. Place the boat back on the trailer to make sure the bunks and rollers are properly adjusted.

Leaf Springs:
Depending on the size of your trailer there can be two to five leaves in each spring. Inspect the leaves. They should be curled upward. If they are flat, they've lost their capacity to suspend the trailer and trailer load and should be replaced. If you find any that are broken, take the trailer to a dealer for repair or replacement.

Lights:
Inspect the tow vehicle connectors for rust and corrosion. Clean the prongs and spray them with WD-40 or CRC to ensure a good connection. To ward off moisture, coat all electrical connections, bulb sockets, and splices with petroleum jelly.

Wheels and Hubs:
Prop up one wheel at a time and spin by hand to listen for grinding noises that indicate a problem inside the hub. Grasp the propped wheel with both hands and jiggle it to test for play. Even if there are no problems, you should still lubricate the wheel bearings on a regular basis. If your trailer has bearing protectors, which replace the hub's dust cover with a grease fitting and reservoir, pump new marine grease into the bearing until the spring-loaded piston is approximately 1/8 inch from its seated position.

Lubricating standard bearings requires that you jack up the trailer to remove the wheels and tires. To do this, knock off the dust cap with a couple of light hammer blows. Then remove the cotter pin, axle nut, and the outside bearing. Slide the wheel off the axle and lay it face down. Pry off the grease seal with a screwdriver and lift out the other bearing. Soak both sets in kerosene or some other solvent.

Inspect the rollers to make sure they aren't rusted or pitted. If they are, replace them. You should also replace them if they have a bluish tint, an indication of overheating. Check the hub's outer races for pitting. Replace as necessary. Next, carefully pack the bearings with marine-grade wheel-bearing grease. Also grease the outer races and the hub and replace the inner bearing.

Seat a new grease seal with a couple of hammer taps. Slip the hub and outer bearing onto the axle. Tighten the axle-nut and spin the wheel a couple of times to make sure it's turning freely. (If it isn't, loosen the nut a bit.) Insert a new cotter pin and bend back its arms to lock the nut in place. Replace the dust cover.

Burned-out or broken trailer lights are quite common, but fairly easy to fix or replace.

leaving about ½-inch play in the spring. The Fulton unit is marked to indicating pressure.

Be sure that the transom is secured to the trailer with good transom tie-downs. Such as the EPCO ratchet tie-down or the tie-down from Walk-Winn that features plastic-coated hooks to protect the gelcoat. In some instances you may need to use gunwale tie-downs such as those made by EPCO. My favorites are the BoatBuckle retractable models. They feature a self-storing system when the boat is off the trailer, so you don't have to remove them after launching. They also employ a tightening ratchet. Always make sure your boat bow eye is tightened tight in place as well.

TRAILER LIGHTS AND WIRING

Trailer light repair or installation is not difficult and doesn't require a lot of tools. You'll need an inexpensive multimeter, an electrical tester, a crimping tool and connectors, spare flasher, bulbs, and fuses. The electrical tester has an alligator clip to attach a ground and a probe to test wiring. The tester light glows in the presence of a 12-volt current. The multimeter detects voltage at any point in the circuit. A voltage drop might indicate that larger wiring should be used or that corrosion or loose wiring is impeding the current flow.

If you have a light that isn't working, determine if the bulb or sealed capsule is bad. Broken or burned-out bulbs are fairly evident. If the bulb appears to be ok, determine if there is power to the bulb. First check the bulb with the multimeter for continuity. If the bulb is ok, clean the bulb socket and retest. If the light is still out, check the towing vehicle plug with the electrical tester for a voltage reading. If both show voltage, the problem is in the wiring. Use the sharp probe to work down the defective circuit until a break in voltage is discovered. The problem lies between this point and the last "good" voltage reading.

Another common problem is a poor ground connection through the trailer or tow vehicle frame. Check to ensure that the grounding wire is properly attached. The white ground wire must be firmly joined to both vehicle and trailer frame. See that none of the wires are pinched, incorrectly routed, or have loose connections. If you find a break in a wire, unplug the trailer from the towing vehicle, and cut the wires to remove any worn areas or bare metal. Strip about ¼-inch of insulation and reconnect using a trailer wiring crimp-on type fastener.

If installing an entirely new trailer light harness kit, make sure you read and follow manufacturer's instructions.

Chapter 11

Small Boats

Many of us began our fishing days in Johnboats, and these utilitarian models still provide lots of bass fishing fun.

Although pure bass boats are the ideal for most serious bass anglers, many other types of boats can also do bass-boat duty. And many bass boats can also be used for other types of fishing, as well as for pleasure boating.

JOHNBOATS

Chances are, if you're a serious bass angler, some time in your life you've fished out of a Johnboat. Perhaps it was a traditional wooden boat on a southern river, or a dented and well-worn metal boat on your grandfather's favorite pond. Even with the popularity of big, glittery, fast and high-tech bass boats, old-fashioned Johnboats still provide plenty of opportunities for getting to some of the best bass angling in the country – the backwaters, sloughs, ponds, small rivers, and small lakes where the big boats can't go.

Johnboats have the advantage that they don't require a lot of horsepower, even the bigger ones. They are ideal for many of the smaller community lakes that are limited to electric power only. Another reason for the popularity of Johnboats is the same as always – they're extremely economical, with a little care they'll last a lifetime – sometimes more than one.

Major factors in the renewed popularity of Johnboats are better materials

Any number of small boat types can be rigged as bass boats including this classic aluminum John boat.

and construction, improved hull designs, better interior layouts, and a wide range of available accessories. A number of companies produce a range of sizes, from tiny 8-footers you can slide into your pickup to huge models over 20 feet long that can carry huge loads of gear and people.

Johnboats of the past had flat bottoms and a slightly turned up square bow. These were great for moving slow in protected, shallow waters, but they offered a pounding, wet ride on anything more than a calm, smooth surface.

Newer boats include shallow, semi-V bows, which cut the water providing a softer and drier ride. Some Johnboats are built with an increasingly sharper dead rise, flared bow, and even more pronounced chines for smoother rides and better handling. Many companies produce tunnel hull models for use with jet power units for operation in extremely shallow water, or for fishing coastal waters and flats. The OMC Aluminum Boat Group Rough-neck 16- and 17-foot tunnel models are specifically set up for jet-drive outboards. An optional saddle fuel tank also properly positions the center of gravity for optimum shallow water performance.

Johnboats are commonly constructed of aluminum in gauges ranging from .054 inch for small, economical car-toppers to .125 inch for the bigger, better quality models. Boats can be of riveted or welded construction. Welded

models, generally provide superior strength and durability, and come with a greater variety of interior configurations. The higher-quality boats will also have stronger one-piece, extruded ribs and reinforced corner and transom braces. Another mark of the quality Jon boat is reinforcing in major use areas, such as front decks and rear seats. This allows for installation of pedestal seat bases. Some of the better models also offer foam flotation under the seats, decks and other selected areas.

Most Johnboats come in the same dull, drab, army-brown of yesteryear, with enamel paint simply sprayed on. It doesn't take long for these boats to get a "well-worn" look. Many of the higher-quality boats, however, utilize baked-on finishes in a variety of colors. The Lowe Roughneck Series features CamoClad, Mossy Oak Breakup, and Advantage Wetlands camouflage on all models. War Eagle finishes the complete interior of their boats in brand-name camo (Mossy Oak Bottomland, Treestand, Shadow Grass, Break up and Advantage Wetlands).

SeaArk produces an interior coating called Gatorhide as an

option. This coating, available in several colors is a high-density urethane that deadens sound and adds a non-slip, protective surface to the boat interior. Gatorhide is gas and chemical resistant and is easy to wash down and clean.

INTERIOR ARRANGEMENTS AND OPTIONS

The design of the basic Jon boat easily allows you to rig the interior to suit your own needs. You can add almost anything from a home-built fishing deck to high-tech livewells and modular storage. Pedestal and removable seats can also be added as desired. Several Johnboat models come with "the basics" which provides a very comfortable fishing boat at a very economical price. A good example are the SeaArk "P" models. Ranging in length from 15 to 18 feet, they all come with an extended bow deck with a stainless steel seat base plate. There's also a storage box under the bow deck, an extra-wide rear seat with stainless steel base plate, a console with aerated livewell, an aerator pump, a console with wiring, and

Some of the first bass boats were stick-steer. This feature is still common on several 15 -16-foot models.

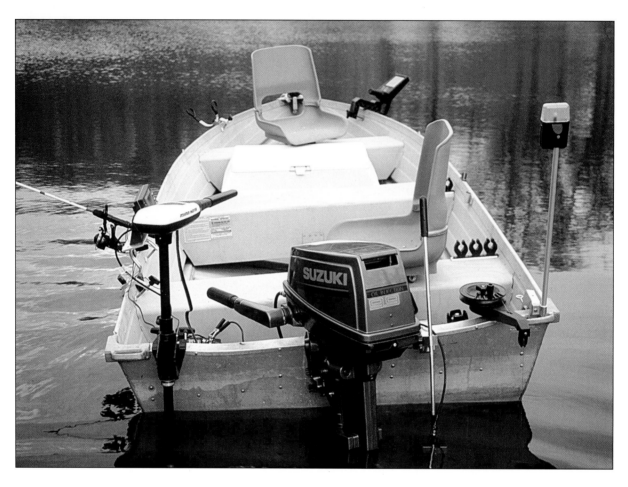

a shift control bracket. Pedestal fishing seats and a center console are options.

The Grizzly models from Tracker Marine include the Grizzly Bass, specifically laid out for bass fishing with a center aerated livewell, rod storage and front and rear fishing seats. The package includes bow storage, dual rod holders and a stick steer front seat. A fishing rig includes the Tracker 12-volt, 43-pound thrust, 36-inch shaft foot-controlled trolling motor, battery and battery tray.

Alumacraft, one of the nation's premier Johnboat builders, offers a deluxe version of several of their boats. Standard features include a center or side console, aluminum floor, light package, bilge pump, and trolling motor harness with plug and receptacle.

Johnboats are now available with all kinds of options. SeaArk offers livewells, a center console with windshield and livewell along with a flats poling platform, a seat extrusion with a high-rise adapter, a fold-down camo seat, a side

console, extended deck, a gun box, a half seat and even a four-wheeler ramp.

Options on the Lowe boats include a Bimini top and side-mounted polyethylene storage boxes that can be converted into 46-quart gravity fed livewells. Options on some models include a floor liner, adjustable steering console, and trolling motor mount. One of the more unusual options comes with the Roughneck all-welded series. The Accessory Receiver Gunwale features a slot to hold matching accessories with mount brackets that snap in place along the gunwale rail. These include a fish finder, rod rack, storage box, engine-gauge panel and rod holders.

Flooring can be a useful option on a Johnboat. If nothing else, adding a floor increases the ease of use deadens the sound and provides a safer boat, as you don't have exposed ribs to stumble over. The floor, available either as an option or standard on certain models covers the cross ribs. Crestliner provides a skid-resistant coating to their floors.

STICK STEER BOATS

Some of the first bass boats were steered by pushing a stick forward or pulling it back. With the race toward faster bass boats with bigger engines, stick steering became "obsolete." Driving today's high-speed bass boats would be extremely dangerous with a stick. On lower powered boats, however, stick steering is a viable option that offers a number of advantages. The driver is seated close to the bow. The stick steering mechanism is located on the port side of the boat and the engine throttle/shift mechanism is placed as usual on the starboard side. Both are within arm's reach on the inside of the gunwales. This limits stick steering to relatively small boats.

A number of small, aluminum, stick steer models are available.

They are lightweight, shallow-draft, sturdy, go-anywhere boats that are right at home on small, protected waters, backwater sloughs, rivers and stump-riddled shallow waters. With the driver seated forward, visibility is excellent. Weight is more evenly distributed, allowing boats to run shallower than with all the weight in the stern.

Sitting forward offers another advantage. When you shut down the motor you're ready to fish – just grab your rod and start casting. Stick steer models are great for older and less agile anglers because they don't have to get up from behind a console and step up on a deck to begin casting. In fact, once driver and passenger are seated in a stick steer boat they don't have to get up except to reach items in the center of the boat.

Trolling from a stick steer is extremely easy, and sitting forward offers the opportunity to add spider rigging for several rods right off the bow. Stick steer boats make excellent craft for small rivers and bodies of water. Because of their compact lightweight engines, stick steer boats are easy to tow and operate. Many come with built-in livewells, and they can be rigged with all the amenities of a serious bass fishing machine. You can even rig a stick steer with a jet engine for the ultimate in shallow-water access. Although many have ratings for several people, they're really best as "two-person" boats.

With their growing popularity, a number of stick steer models are

available with Tracker Marine offering three models. Tracker offers three excellent models: the 16-foot Grizzly Bass; 15-foot, 10-inch, Panfish 16; and the 16-foot, three-inch Fisher 16 Dominator SS. Xpress offers a great "bare-bones" stick steer in their 15-foot 1546CPXY. The riveted aluminum McCrappie 15 from SeaArk is also an excellent little 15-footer. Lowe offers the 162, a 16-foot Panfish with a 71-inch beam in a standard package with 10EL Johnson engine and bunk trailer. Ranger offers the 116ST Stick Steer Cherokee. It's 16-feet with a 78-inch beam, has a 40 horsepower rating, and 5/1082 weight rating.

JET BOATS

Jet powered boats allow you to get into places otherwise fairly inaccessible. This includes ankle-deep water, white-water rapids, over sandbars, shoals and other shallow-water obstacles that will mangle both prop and lower unit. Misused, however, jet-drives can damage delicate streams and water systems. Used with proper environmental attention, jets are great for shallow-water anglers.

Jet-drives have been popular in some regions for a long time, especially in the Pacific Northwest where trout and salmon fishermen have used them in the white-water rivers of Alaska, Oregon, and Washington. Jets have become popular in other regions as well. In 1994 Roland Martin used a

prop engine – and they consume up to three times as much fuel. The jet lower unit is also quite a bit heavier than a prop unit, adding to the rear-end weight of a boat. Jets have poor out-of-the-hole shot performance and the intake can suck up debris.

Naturally the best boats for jet-drives are lightweight, aluminum models. But they should be solid and well made to handle the abuse shallow water and especially shoals, sandbars and other obstacles dish out. Johnboats, available in sizes from 14 to 20 feet long, are the most commonly used jet boats, as are aluminum boats especially designed to handle the Pacific Northwest white-water rivers. Any number of manufacturers offer excellent models.

You can add even more shallow water ability, and also cut down on the blowout, with the use of a tunnel hull boat such as the Roughneck boats from the OMC Aluminum Boat Group. Available in both 16- and 17-foot models, the design places the water intake a full three inches above the hull bottom. Underwater obstacles are less likely to strike the jet-drive lower unit.

DECK BOATS AND PONTOONS

Deck boats and pontoons, often considered "party" boats, can also do double duty as "bass" boats. Decks and pontoons offer group fun. If you want to take your kids

Ranger Cherokee with a Mercury jet outboard to fish a hard-to-get-to spot of the Connecticut River to win a B.A.S.S. tournament.

Jets are quite simple and have a minimum number of moving parts. Water is drawn into the unit through an intake grille by an engine-driven impeller. The water is then forced at high pressure through an outlet nozzle that is directed away from the stern. To reverse, a gate swings to block the outlet, directing the pressure stream in the opposite direction. Inboard and outboard jet-drives are available. The most common are standard outboard engines with special jet lower units available from Mercury, OMC, and Yamaha. They range from 20 to 115 horsepower.

Jet power drives also have some cons. Running up on plane in open water with a chop creates a "blow out." Each time the jet nozzle bounces out of the water there is less pressure, and the boat stalls and catches repeatedly. Current jet-drive manufacturers have worked hard to reduce this problem. Jet drives are also less efficient than propped engines by about 25 to 30 percent – you need a 75 horsepower jet to equal the power of a 50 horsepower or grandkids fishing, you just can't beat a deck boat or a pontoon. They usually have plenty of freeboard with a lowered deck in deck boats, or safety railings on pontoons.

Deck boats, primarily designed for family water recreation, are becoming more "angler friendly." SeaArk has three deck boat models, the Sun Tastic, Sun Star and Sun King, all 20 feet, one inch. Anglers will appreciate the two, removable, fold-down fishing chairs located on the forward deck along with an 11-gallon aerated livewell located between the seats. Lockable rod or ski storage is located in the floor. All three models are available with a fish package that includes a Lowrance X-25 depth finder and Motor-Guide 750 Brute trolling motor.

Pontoons offer even more roomy fishability, and Tracker Marine has several excellent models including their Fishin' Barge 25 and 21 as well as the Bass Buggy 18. The "Barges" come with lockable rod and tackle storage. All three models have two pedestal bow fishing seats along with an aerated livewell system. All are pre-wired for a trolling motor.

The PlayCraft Sunfish 2400 Troller pontoon features two front fishing seats, two rear fishing seats, and is pre-wired for trolling motor with panel and plug. The front corner caps have drink holders and built-in tackle trays and a surface mount fish finder and aerated livewell add to the fishability. The PlayCraft Fishdeck FX 4 com-

bines the best of both worlds with a fiberglass hull for performance and smooth ride, along with the spaciousness of a pontoon deck.

SMALL BOATS

Raised on a farm near Clinton, Missouri, well before the huge reservoirs dotted our countryside, I grew up fishing the numerous farm ponds owned by my relatives and neighbors as well as the old flooded strip mines in the area. I quickly learned that the best fishing usually wasn't from the bank, even on small ponds and that bank fishing was almost impossible in the strip pits. So I built a small plywood dinghy using plans from *Popular Mechanics* magazine, and have been hooked on boats for big and small waters ever since.

Uncounted numbers of small bodies of water exist throughout the country, often close to major population centers. These waters include farm ponds, community lakes, wildlife-management areas, abandoned strip mines, and small and medium streams. One of the largest stringers of big bass I've ever caught came several years ago out of such a community lake in northern Missouri. Backcountry small waters include beaver ponds and natural lakes, bayous, swamps, and rivers. All of these, as well as coves on reservoirs and bays on lakes, offer plenty of bass fishing opportunities.

Many community lakes and wildlife management areas have motor regulations that limit outboard motors to 10 horsepower or smaller. Some of these small bodies of water have ramps with fairly easy access, but others are often located well off the main roads, and have no ramp access. Car topping is a favorite method for getting a small, lightweight boat into these overlooked fishing hotspots.

Small-sized motor and boat packages offer several other advantages – especially cost. You can get into a fishing package very inex-

Fiberglass baby boats will fit inside a pickup, are sized to carry two people, and are often powered by small trolling motors.

pensively by choosing a small boat and motor. Small boats are economical to maintain and operate and take up less storage space In addition they are easily transported and handled. With a little care and careful maintenance they'll provide a lifetime of use.

Small boats come in several sizes and types, including aluminum John and utility boats, canoes, folding and inflatable boats as well as "baby" bass boats. Following are some of the the basic types and a discussion of their various advantages and disadvantages.

FOLDING BOATS

If you're short on space for storage, a folding boat, such as the Porta-Bote, is an excellent choice. Available in 10- and 12-foot models, the Porta-Bote is constructed of extra-strong polypropylene, folds down flat to four inches thick and unfolds, ready to use, in just a few minutes. Available in white or duck hunter green, the folded boat can be strapped to an RV, slid in the back of a pickup, or car topped. Options include a removable sun shade.

INFLATABLE BOATS

Inflatables, now available with rigid bottoms of either wood or molded plastic, can also be extremely good farm pond boats. Some inflatable boats require a bit of time in assembling, but are extremely maneuverable. The Zodiak Fish 'n' Hunt is designed just for fishing and hunting, and comes with a livewell seat and an optional blind that converts the boat into a dandy duck boat for small waters. The Float 'n' Tote is a hybrid inflatable, using the advantages of an inflatable boat and a float tube. You sit in the boat with your feet dangling in the water, and it can be propelled like a float tube with flippers or rowed with the aluminum oars. These are the lightest in weight for lifting around or dragging down to the water's edge. They don't have the life span of aluminum or fiberglass constructed boats, but many do have transoms for small motors.

"BABY" BASS BOATS

Several years ago a lawyer, dressed in one of the fanciest suits you can imagine, sat down next to me on an airplane as I was coming back from a fishing assignment. He proceeded to open a bass fishing magazine and read. I couldn't help but point out that I was the author of one of the articles in the magazine. With that he immediately dug into his $500 brief case and came out with a stack of bonzo bass photos that would make any bass pro cry like a baby. His secret? A couple of suburban lakes in the Chicago area. Not

overly large, the lakes were restricted to electric trolling motors, and he used a tiny, two-man baby bass boat with a front-mounted motor. "I guess I'll eventually want one of those big honkers," he said as he pointed to the latest full-size bass boat ad in the magazine. "But not while I'm catching fish like this, and right near my home."

That's the advantage two-man, and even one-man, bass boats offer. You can fish these boats in places you can't get other boats. Baby bass boats are basically one- or two-man boats of fiberglass or ABS plastic formed in two pieces. The lower half consists of two pontoons and a hull. The deck has a floor, gunwales, trolling motor mounts and other molded-in features. Sliding and/or swivel seats are positioned in place. These baby bass boats offer more comfort than many Jon boats and utility boats, and can be pulled around by a bow-mounted trolling motor or pushed with a transom mount, if preferred. They can also be picked up and slid into the back of a pickup or utility vehicle.

SMALL MOTORS

While many of the smaller boats can easily be paddled or rowed, an electric trolling motor, which can be located either fore or aft, is a very popular method of propulsion. Tiny outboard motors can also be used. Choosing the proper outboard motor and matching the proper motor to a small boat is extremely important. A wide variety of small motor sizes are available on the market. While the definition of a small motor can vary, they usually range in size and power rating from the tiny 2.5 up to 9.9 horsepower. The 15-, 20-, and even 25-horsepower engines can also be considered small motors in some cases. If the boat is to be stored on a trailer and you don't have to worry about removing your motor after every fishing trip, you'll probably want the most powerful "small" motor you can match to the boat. Even the 9.9s (around 70 pounds) can be hefty and awkward to lift and transport, so you may prefer a smaller, lighter weight motor if your boat is hand lifted.

Chapter 12

Buy, Finance, Insure and Secure Your Investment

Buying a bass boat is a major decision. Before shopping, make a list of features you will need in a boat that best suits your fishing style.

*B*ass boats are a major investment. Buying, financing, insuring, and securing that investment are important factors in owning a bass boat of any size. Regardless of whether you are buying a new or used boat, a first consideration is the fact that you are actually buying a "rig." This means a boat, engine, boat trailer, trolling motor and accessories, such as electronic depth sounders, fish locators, and numerous other options. If you're ready to buy a bass boat rig, a few buying tips can save you money and headaches later on.

As a prospective bass boat buyer you should know the type of boat you want and can afford. This sounds simple enough, but impulse buying happens, especially in the glitter of a showroom and with pressure from salespersons.

Make a list of what boat is right for you. Do you want an alminum or fiberglass boat? Consider the size. If the boat is to be used for tournaments, make sure you get a boat that's big enough to handle rough water. The boat should also be maneuverable and comfortable to drive. Consider the horsepower of the engine best suited to your fishing applications. If you plan to fish competitively, remember that some professional fishing circuits have horsepower limits. Also, list the optional equipment you want, such as trolling motor, electronics, high-capacity bilge pumps and the like. To compare products properly you'll need to compare products equally, realizing that there is more to comparison than price.

When you have narrowed the field to the boats that fit your requirements, ask your dealers to price those boats equally. This means without engine, rigging charges, and engine accessory equipment. You'll probably find there isn't much difference in price between the best boats on the market.

If there is a difference in the price of the basic boats, you need to question what accounts for that difference. For instance, on fiber-glass boats look first at the finish and glance down the side against the light. Good solid hull lay-up means no wavy-looking surfaces. It's the little things that make up the fit and finish that are good indications of overall quality. Thump your fist against the side of the boat. A solid feel and sound is an indication of strength and durability. It also means the boat will fish quietly, even in choppy water.

Because all boats are built of separately molded parts, look for a boat with the feel of a "one-piece" boat. It should be firmly glassed together for safety and longevity as well as be rigid and not flexing. Examine welds on aluminum boats. Are there rough spots or other indications of poor craftsmanship?

Never skimp on the foam flotation material and always check on how and where the material is used. Other safety considerations might be a no-feedback steering setup.

Check out the storage. Does the boat have enough storage for your needs? Are the storage compartments lockable and easy to access? Also consider whether you want a single or dual console. Many anglers fish at husband-and-wife or buddy tournaments, and the dual console models offer greater comfort for fishing part-ners.

Performance is an all-inclusive word. It's often misunderstood as meaning only speed, but per-formance also includes handling comfort, fishability, reliability and customer confidence. Some boats run fast but fish poorly. They lack the ride that gives you the confi-dence of safety under all water conditions. Tournament fishermen are particularly conscious of this, and use those boats that will "get you there and back" under the

Did You Know?
Boat Shopping Tips

The first thing to do is to make a list of your needs and take the list with you when you go boat shopping.

A. Types of lakes and rivers you fish--deep, shallow, stumps, rocky, large, small, etc.

B. Your style of fishing--trolling, casting, flipping.

C. Tournament or weekend angler--mostly yourself, you and a partner, family, etc.

D. Will the boat be used for family pleasure boating as well as fishing? If so, how many people and what activities?

E. How far do you travel to fish?

F. Size of your tow vehicle.

G. Storage space available for your boat.

H. Purchase budget, including amount of monthly payment.

I. Operating budget of boat, including insurance.

demanding requirements of their sport.

Different styles and sizes of boats drive differently. Ask your dealer about a possible test drive. It is well worth even the cost of a long trip to try out that boat before buying. Test drive with the family or fishing partner, to make sure seating and/or fishability suits everyone involved.

Your comparison list now indi-cates that there is more to consid-er than you may have expected when boat shopping. The old saying, "you get what you pay for" " holds true, particularly as it applies to quality, reputation, and resale value. A smart approach will turn your expenditure into an investment. The return on this investment translates into pride in ownership, the best service for your product, and the most resale value when you trade. That's how you shop for boats.

COST

Be aware that some purchase costs are hidden. Freight and dealer rigging costs are often added to the initial sticker price. Depending on where you live and how far the boat must be shipped, the shipping price can be fairly expensive. Some boat packages include electronics, others don't. The more you add in the way of electronics, naturally the more the cost, not only of the equipment but also in the rigging. You must also pay sales tax, and with many of today's boats approaching $40,000, sales tax is not cheap.

If you purchase a boat on a payment plan, the interest cost should be added. It pays to shop around for the lowest interest rates. With the high cost of today's boats, coupled with liability problems, most owners insure their boats – another cost. In most cases when you're buying on time, the lender will require that you purchase insurance.

Remember, it is expensive to own a boat. The first expense, of course, is operating expense. While some boat and motor combinations are relatively inexpensive to run, others swallow gas in gulps. Tests such as those conducted by *Bass & Walleye Boats Magazine* give information on gas consumption that can be a major help in choosing a boat.

Maintenance is another often ignored cost of boat ownership. Boats do require regular maintenance. Following regular maintenance schedules on engines saves money in the long run. You should also ask the dealer about ease of working on or in the boat. Are electric components, fuses, wiring harnesses, and especially bilge and livewell pumps and hoses easily accessible?

Another mistake that can be costly is skimping on the trailer cost in order to purchase a bigger or higher-priced boat. Usually your boat spends more time on the trailer than it does on the water, and in some cases you spend as much or more time pulling your boat as driving it. Quality trailers fitted to your boat and with amenities and safety features such as brakes, dual wheels, and tilt tongue are important.

Finally, warranties are extremely important. In shopping for your investment, make sure you understand what is covered and for how long. Boat, motor, trolling motor, accessories and trailer may have separate warranties. Check out the warranty on each component of your rig. A good idea is to purchase only a National Marine Manufacturers Association

(NMMA)-certified boat. According to U.S. Coast Guard statistics, boat buyers can feel five times safer when they purchase a boat that is certified by NMMA.

BUYING A USED BOAT

Quality used boats are available, but like used cars, it takes some astute shopping as well as some sharp horse-trading to get a bargain. The amount of warranty left on the boat, motor, and accessories is important, as is the general condition. Make sure you thoroughly inspect the boat, engine, trolling motor, accessories, and trailer. Make the same list as mentioned in "Boat Shopping Tips" when hunting for a used boat.

Inspecting a Used Boat
Walk around the boat and inspect for cracks or gouges in fiberglass or deep dents, broken welds or loose rivets in aluminum boats. A few battle scars, such as chips or scratches in gelcoat or scraped paint on aluminum boats are ok, but the boat should be structurally sound. Pay particular attention to the transom particularly where it joins the sides of the hull. Major damage in this area means major repair work. Tilt the motor all the way up, then push down on the lower unit. There should be no flexing of the transom. Make a thorough inspections of all wiring, making sure there are no breaks or corrosion and that all of the connections are solid.

Above all else, insist on a test ride. During this test you can check for soundness of steering and throttle control. Try out the trolling motor, the bilge and livewell pumps, and the lights. Check out the bilge area to determine if the boat is taking on water. Once back on the trailer, thoroughly inspect the bottom to make sure there is no major through-hull damage. You will also be able to determine if there are major leaks because water will drip from cracks or gouges.

Engine

Unless you're a pretty good mechanic, the best bet is to have a qualified marine mechanic check out the engine. This could be your best insurancein buying a used boat. If you have the skills and equipment you can do the chores yourself, making sure you check engine compression, proper carburetor or fuel injection operation, the ignition system, the water pump and the lower unit gear case.

Trailer

Inspect the coupler, chains, winch and winch stand, dolly and the entire frame for damages, loose, or missing, parts. Inspect the bunks. Determine if they need re-carpeting or if the carpeting needs to be refastened. Also, are they sagging, indicating rotten or weak support boards? Jack up the trailer, spin the wheels and check the wheel bearings. Inspect all lights and wiring to determine if they are working.

FINANCING

As with purchasing, you should shop around for financing for your new or used boat. In many instances the dealer or manufacturer may offer financing. You should also check with your local banker or credit union, to determine if a better deal is available. Boat loans are also available over the Internet. Even if you're not ready to borrow money over the Internet, many websites offer loan calculators that would give you a

good idea of the cost. Visiting one of these websites before shopping would let you know how much you could afford to spend on your boat package. These websites will also give you the rates available for boat loans, numbers that you can use to compare with other loan offers.

Depending on your credit rating, as much as 90 percent of the purchase price of a new boat can be financed. This purchase price can also include everything added to the boat at the time of purchase, such as trolling motor and electronics, as well as upgrades to packaged boat rigs. Pre-approval of a boat-purchasing loan is another option. With a pre-approved loan you know up front how much you can spend, and when you find the best deal you're ready to buy.

Don't forget the important fac-

Understanding Insurance

The National Boat Owner's Association suggests several steps to keep your insurance premiums as low as possible:

1. Complete an authorized boating course.

2. Inspect or have your boat inspected by a qualified marine mechanic at least twice a year.

3. Repair or replace defective equipment promptly.

4. Have a well-thought-out, written plan to carry out in the event of a natural disaster.

5. Store your boat in a secure area. Install theft-prevention devices on all electronics, outboard engines, trailer hitches, trailer hitch receivers, trailer wheels, etc.

6. Install alarm systems in all boats stored in the water. These systems should at the least warn against high bilge water levels and cabin intrusion by unauthorized persons.

7. Follow responsible activities, such as using PFDs, limiting alcohol consumption, following rules of the road, observing speed limits and no-wake signs, taking refueling precautions, etc.

tors for any loan prepayment and the total cost of the loan. Low monthly payments can sound good, but those lower payments are usually on longer-term loans. The total cost of that long-term loan can be a lot more than a shorter-term loan with a higher monthly payment. Don't forget that your lender will require full-coverage insurance on your rig for the entire length of the loan.

INSURANCE

Back in the old days, many sport-fishing boats were relatively cheap. These days it's not unusual for a fully rigged bass boat to run close to $40,000. Our waters have become more crowded as well, and the chances of a boating accident increase with the crowds. Having the correct boat insurance these days has become a necessity. But, not all insurance is the same. Different boats and different situations require different types of insurance.

First, determine if you need insurance. As I've said, if you're borrowing money to purchase a boat, the lender will require comprehensive coverage in case of damage to their property, and with litigation the norm today, it also pays to insure for liability.

Although most insurance companies will insure a boat, you may wish to look into agencies that specialize in marine insurance, such as through the National Boat Owner's Association. Again, you

can shop for and purchase insurance via the Internet. You may also wish to check with local agencies for a comparison of prices and coverage. Arlene Lear, an independent agent, suggests the best way to shop for any insurance, including marine insurance, is through an independent agency that represents several companies.

Arlene also suggests that you be aware of the pitfalls and traps that might occur when buying insurance from an agent or company unfamiliar with boats. One pitfall to avoid is not listing all possible drivers, to prevent liability problems later. If you comparison-shop, you will find that some carriers are better than others. For instance, some agencies will give as much as a 25 percent discount if they also have coverage on your autos or home. It's also best to always stay with an A-rated or better company.

The types of coverage you may consider include: liability on and off the water; property coverage on boat, motors, trailer and equipment; medical payments and possibly uninsured and underinsured boater coverage. If you have an older boat and don't have a lot of money invested in it, you may decide to forgo the property and collision coverage. On the other hand, even with an older boat, when you start adding up depth finders, GPS, a dozen or so rods, tackle and other gear, you may find insuring your property is a good idea. Make sure you know what is covered in the policy in regards to gear and equipment on and in the boat and where the boat is stored. A $250 deductible policy is usually the best for the price. A surcharge is usually added for a smaller deductible and there is very little savings on premiums for a higher deductible.

Make sure you have road coverage when trailering your boat. Most companies automatically extend liability from the towing vehicle, but not always. It is always important to let your insurance carrier know you're towing a trailer of any kind. Also, liability extended from an auto policy does not provide coverage while on the water. On-the-water coverage must be insured separately either by extending coverage from your homeowner's policy or by purchasing a separate policy.

Above all else, before signing on the dotted line, make sure you read and understand your insurance policy thoroughly. Know what is insured and what isn't. You may have to list all the equipment to be covered in your policy. And, if you list equipment, make sure you keep the list updated. An annual insurance update is a good idea for all types of insurance.

BOAT AND TRAILER PROTECTION

The next step is to prevent someone from stealing your boat and trailer from your vehicle – or your trailer while you're out on the lake. If your tow vehicle has a removable ball hitch mechanism

held by a pin, the Gorilla Guard Receiver Lock from Fulton can be used to secure the receiver. Gorilla Guard also has a Trailer Lock that locks the ball in place on your hitch. And, finally, there's the Trailer Hitch Lock from Fulton that fits through the lift handle pin-hole on ball hitch couplers. The Safe-T-Hitch from Flushette Manufacturing bolts in place between the hitch ball and the bumper plate. The ball shank acts as the securing bolt. After the trailer tongue is placed on the hitch ball, the top slides over and is secured with a bolt or padlock, making it impossible to lift the trailer tongue off the hitch ball.

The next step is securing your trailer while it's off your vehicle. Leaving the coupler lock in place so the lift handle can't be lifted is the first step. The Trailock uses a key and bar system to lock the trailer wheel in place and prevent it from turning. Installation is quick and easy. The user simply replaces the lug nuts with Trailock universal steel hex adapters, then adds the steel back plate. These parts of the system remain on the wheel, and don't interfere with the trailer's operation. The Fulton Trailer Keeper is a steel locking device that attaches to lug latches on a case-hardened steel rod which is threaded through the wheel and tire. The lug latches are secured to the wheel lock bar with a special brass padlock.

The Gorilla Guard vinyl-coated steel cable with cable lock or cable lock combination can be

used to secure the trailer to a solid item such as post.

RIGGING AND GEAR PROTECTION

The next step is to prevent items from being removed from your trailer and boat. The Fulton Gorilla Guard Spare Tire Lock fits over wheel studs and has a key-locking cap to deter spare-tire

theft. The Wesbar Locking Spare Tire Carrier consists of a mounting bracket with two threaded spokes to fit around the trailer frame. The spare tire slides onto the spokes and screws in place. Locking bars on either side of the tire are clamped together by a heavy-duty padlock.

You can prevent removal of your outboard motor with a Fulton Outboard Motor Lok, which mounts on most outboard motor clamps. This unit has a key lock, heavy-gauge steel body and foam filler insert to reduce noise and vibration.

Prevention of electronic theft is easy – simply remove the units. Take them with you, or lock them in your vehicle or boat if you must leave your boat exposed. Most units

are made to detach easily, but you can also mount them with fast-removal mounting systems, such as the Ultra Mount from T & L Products or Round-A-Mount Systems from National Products.

Although most trolling motors are bolted in place and somewhat hard to remove, quick-detachable trolling motor mounts are available that allow you to easily remove the motor. They include the Swivl-Eze Trol-Lock and the JWA Quick Release PowerDrive Mount Bracket, which allows quick removal of any Minn Kota PowerDrive or AutoPilot unit. You can also lock your transom mount Minn Kota trolling motor in place with their Transom Lock. Pinpoint trolling motors and plug-in bow-mount LCD units can both be

very quickly removed from your boat and reinstalled in seconds. Most quality bass boats have lockable compartments for gear and tackle. If you wish to add more locks, there are water-tight, recessed locks available for aluminum, fiberglass and composite lids from T-H Marine.

BOAT SECURITY SYSTEMS

Auto alarm systems have been available for years, and now boat owners can purchase systems designed specifically to protect their boats and gear.

The Kombi Gard alarm from ThermeX alerts owners to craft tampering with noise and flashing lights. It also prevents a boat's engine from being started. It includes a control unit which operates off the boat's 12-volt power source, regulated with a microprocessor driver with four separate alarm sections. The four magnet contacts can be mounted in different parts of the craft, to signal intrusion in a specific protected area.

When activated, a siren sounds for 40 seconds. Next, the running lights, or a separate flashing light, will blink for four minutes. An interlock connected to the craft's ignition and starter solenoid prevents the engine from being started after the alarm is activated. The Kombi Gard is controlled by either a key or an optional remote-control unit.

The C.O.P. line of boat security systems, which stands for Constant On-Shore Protection, is similar to car antitheft devices. It sounds a penetrating, 120-decibel alarm, to ward off would-be thieves or vandals. "We've developed what we believe is the first low-cost, high-tech security system for protecting a boat at dockside or hitched to a tow vehicle," said Ron Sundborg, president of C.O.P. Corporation. "Boat security has become even more serious the

last 10 to 15 years with all the costly electronics and fishing gear people pack into them."

The two models in the line are called the Undercover C.O.P. and Dock C.O.P. The Undercover model features a tension-sensitive loop that can easily be threaded through the drawstring or elastic hem of a boat cover. As soon as someone reaches under the cover or removes it, the alarm goes off. The wiring in the unit is designed to fit covers for boats up to 21 feet long. The sensitivity of the device can be adjusted by the owner, who can also arm the system while the boat is being pulled down the road. A remote control is used to arm or disarm the system from up to 100 feet and features a panic button to attract attention in an emergency. The unit draws only 12 milliamps from the boat's battery and can be installed in minutes.

The Dock C.O.P. can be mounted in an open area of a boat. When armed, it generates an electromagnetic energy field to create what Sundborg calls "a zone of protection." When someone disturbs the zone, the noise is almost deafening. The alarm will blast for 60 seconds, then it automatically rearms itself. Intrusion

sensitivity is set at the factory to prevent triggering by small animals or birds. Like the Undercover model, this unit can also be armed or disarmed remotely from up to 100 feet and features the panic button for attracting attention in an emergency. The Dock C.O.P. unit draws just 20 milliamps from the boat's battery.

HOME SECURITY

If you park your boat and trailer outside near your house or garage, or in your backyard, adding security lighting systems can help deter thieves. Motion-activated lighting is the most economical and uses passive infrared sensors. Dusk-to-dawn lights feature a built-in photo control to automatically turn the lights on at dusk and off at dawn. The Regent Lighting Floodlight with indoor alarm is a twin floodlight capable of detecting motion from up to 70 feet, over a 190-degree field of view. When motion is detected, the light is activated and an indoor control module sounds an alarm and/or turns on an interior lamp that is plugged into the module. The indoor alarm can also be set to sound when motion is detected during the day.

Chapter 13

Boat and Trailer Handling Skills

Launching and loading can be an easy chore or a total embarrassment. Practice how to do it properly away from a busy launch ramp.

John was pouring milk over the youngster's cereal when the horn honked in the driveway. "Gotta run," he yelled as he grabbed the coffee thermos, scooped up a handful of rods and a tackle box, then headed for the front door. Halfway there he turned back and kissed the tousled little head busy slurping cereal to the tune of the Saturday morning cartoon on the kitchen TV. "Have a good day and be careful," his wife called sleepily from the bathroom. "I will," John returned. "See you after dark." But he didn't.

"Toughest job I ever had," related the water patrolman. "Telling Susan that night. You know, we all three went to high school together. John and I sometimes fished together when we both had a day off. He couldn't afford a boat yet but was dreaming about the one he was going to buy. We guess they hit a log in the early morning fog. No life jackets and the kill switch wasn't hooked up. His buddy made it, but John didn't. Prop nearly cut him in half. Now he's just a statistic in my book--no longer a friend and occasional fishing buddy."

Don't become a statistic! Know all of the the basic skills of boat and trailer handling, including towing, launching, driving and retrieving. Always follow all boating and driving safety rules. Make sure you have proper safety equipment aboard, including personal flotation devices, and use it. Don't exceed the limitations of your skills or the boat. Understand the dangers of water hazards and know how to avoid or handle them.

TRAILERING

The first step to a day of fishing is getting your bass boat to the water. Several important safety rules must be followed. Matching the proper size trailer and boat to the tow vehicle is of utmost importance. Do not exceed the manufacturer's vehicle tow rating (available at your local automobile dealer). Towed weight of the trailer is determined by the combined weight of the boat, trailer, motor and gear hauled. Local marine dealers can provide this information. Both tow vehicle ratings and weights are also available from the various manufacturers' websites. You might want to add a towing package to your tow vehicle for better handling and performance. A most important safety step is to thoroughly inspect the trailer once you have attached it to the tow vehicle. Make sure the coupler is down properly and that the safety chains are properly hooked in place. Cross the chains under the trailer tongue. If they're too long, give them a couple of twists to keep them from dragging. Check the tire pressure and make sure the lights are hooked up and working. Ensure that the winch strap and boat tie-downs are secure. Get in your tow vehicle and make sure the mirrors are properly adjusted.

Most tow vehicles and quality bass boat trailers these days make towing a breeze. First timers, however, should make short practice runs – never forget the boat is behind you! Avoid sudden stops and maneuvers. Remember that your tow vehicle not only has to slow itself, but also several thousand pounds of boat and trailer. Leave plenty of room ahead, behind, and beside you on the road. Don't cut corners too tight. Running over curbs or cutting corners can damage the sidewalls of your tires, not to mention bend the trailer frame and cause damage to the boat.

Boating and trailering require basic skills and the determination to follow a set of basic safety rules.

LAUNCHING AND LOADING

Most pro and weekend bass tournament anglers are pretty sharp at boat ramp etiquette, mostly because they have to be. I've watched over 400 boats launched within an hour's time during a Charger Owner's Tournament and watched the efficiency of ramp "sergeants" at B.A.S.S. Tournaments as well. It's usually when you mix in the less experienced recreational boaters that problems begin. They park on the end of the ramp, then begin getting their boat ready for the water, hauling stuff down from the parking lot, and in general creating a long line of frustrated boaters. Here's how you can make your day easier, and less of a hassle, while also making other boaters happier.

PRELAUNCH PREPARATION

In the parking lot, before you approach the ramp, or in the case of a long waiting line, begin your prelaunch preparations. First, remove the tie-downs securing the boat. Make sure, however, that you leave the winch line attached to the bow eye. Install or check and tighten all drain plugs. Check livewell drain positions or plugs. Connect fuel lines, and pump the primer bulb a few times to pressurize the fuel line. Turn the motor key very briefly to check motor battery charge, but do not turn the motor on. If I haven't used my boat for some time, before leaving home, I install a water flush hose attachment to the outboard motor water intake and turn it on for a minute or two, ensuring it will start. Sitting on a boat ramp with a motor that won't start can be extremely frustrating to you and everyone around you.

Move coolers, fishing gear, personal flotation devices (PFDs) and other equipment you may have in your automobile to your boat. Lay out the PFDs and make sure you have enough for all passengers. You may also wish to connect the driver's PFD to the engine kill switch if the lanyard is long enough.

If your trailer lights are not waterproof, unplug the wiring harness between the trailer and your tow vehicle. Raise your outboard or stern drive so it won't scrape on the ramp. Next, be sure to tie at least one, and preferably two, docking lines to the boat so that anyone helping you will be able to control the boat after it's launched.

Another step that can prevent a lot of headaches is to check out the ramp before you pull onto it. How steep is it? Is it algae covered, slick or dry? Is it smooth or does it have roughened surfaces for traction? Depending on your tow vehicle, all these factors can be extremely important.

Determine if there is a dock to tie to after you launch the boat, or whether you will need to beach and tie to the bank. You should also check out the parking lot, making sure there is space for you to park. Some ramp areas require parking vehicles and trailers in separate areas.

LAUNCHING

Once you have the trailer and boat in the water, two methods can be used for launching: with or without power. How far you need to back into the water depends on the method chosen, steepness of the ramp and the water depth. With a little experience you'll quickly learn the best positions on ramps that you use frequently. The ShoreLand'r folks suggest that you stop when the step in front of the trailer fender is even with the water level. Then set the parking brake on the vehicle and you're ready to launch.

A properly fitted trailer will allow a boat to launch itself. But be careful on steep ramps, because a roller trailer might launch your boat before you're ready. Either have a friend hold the docking line as you back into the water or secure it to your vehicle or the trailer. It's best to stop, loosen and then unhook the bow eye winch hook just before final entry into the water. One dangerous possibility exists if using the winch rope to launch. If you snap the ratchet mechanism open without a firm grip on the handle, the weight of the boat may pull it back off the trailer quickly, causing the handle to spin rapidly and cause possible injury. In some cases you may

Backup Basics

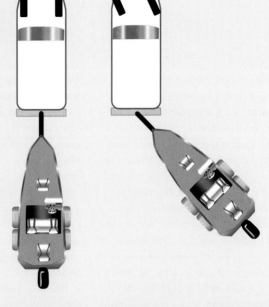

Launch ramp embarrassment is common, and the biggest problem is lack of backing skills. When it's time to launch or retrieve your boat is not the time to practice. You should already have spent a few hours in an empty parking lot polishing your backing skills beforehand. Trying to learn on a launch ramp in front of a group of red-faced and angry boaters who have little interest in helping someone learn on the spot can be frustrating to everyone.

The type of ramp can make backing easy or hard. Wide, single ramps present less problems, but multiple ramps with dividers between the lanes can present real difficulties even for experienced drivers. We have several such ramps on a lake near my home. They were built 40 years ago with concrete dividers between the lanes, and the ramps weren't designed for the wide boats popular these days. There's not much room for error, but it does keep one boater from hogging the entire ramp area.

Follow these steps when launching:

1. Pull onto the ramp apron, if there is one, and make a turn to position the trailer for backing into the water. This usually presents the least amount of backing needed.
2. In some cases, you may be required to back from the parking lot, or even roadway.
3. If at all possible, align the boat trailer with the tow vehicle in a straight line with the boat ramp.
4. Very slowly back the boat trailer and tow vehicle toward the water.
5. Either watch the trailer through your rear window, out the driver's side or use your side mirrors.
6. Most bass boats are low enough for you to see over them, but some are fairly high.
7. In this case back slightly to your left to avoid hitting something in the blind spot behind the rear far corner of the boat and trailer.

There's only one rule to backing a trailer and boat.

The stern of the boat will move in the opposite direction of the tow vehicle's steering wheel. If you turn the steering wheel and the vehicle's front wheels to the left, the stern of the boat will go to the right.

Some drivers like to position their hands at the bottom of the steering wheel, as this reduces confusion in steering. Another common problem in backing is the same as in first learning to drive a vehicle oversteering. Don't turn the wheels sharply; turn them just enough to keep the boat and trailer headed in a straight rearward direction.

Another problem is a ramp that doesn't have a straight angle to the water but "breaks" over at one point.

1. Backing to launch with your boat on the trailer is usually not a problem because the boat sits high enough that you're able to see the direction of the boat and trailer even when it drops over the angle change.
2. Backing with the trailer for retrieval, however, often results in momentarily losing sight of the trailer.
3. Trailers with side bunk load guides make it easier to see the trailer at all times. Many bass boat trailers have these, but you can also purchase them to add to other trailers. You can also add boat guides such as those from Fulton Performance Products. These boat guides are fully adjustable for all popular trailers, and their 50-inch height makes it easy to see the trailer while backing down sharp ramps. Guides also make it easy to center the boat while driving it onto the trailer.

need to give your boat a slight shove to get it moving backwards, but in most instances it's easier to simply back a bit farther into the water. In low water conditions watch that the ramp doesn't end before the boat floats and your tires drop off into the soft lake bottom.

Launching a boat by power is usually the choice, particularly if fishing with a partner. One drives the vehicle and the other the boat. You can even do this single-handed on some ramps. In any case, leave the winch strap attached to the bow eye until you're actually in the boat, then reach over, snap the switch to off and, making sure you hold firmly to the handle, loosen the winch enough to unsnap the eye and you're ready to launch. I usually like to start the engine before this step. Make sure you have the engine tilted down and there's enough water for prop clearance before a power launch. Then apply power slowly and smoothly, just enough to get the boat moving off the trailer. Once the boat is afloat, quickly tie it to the dock and park the trailer, allowing the next person access to the ramp.

LOADING

Loading your boat onto a properly fitted trailer at the end of the day can be a breeze; with an improperly fitted trailer it can be the single most frustrating situation of the day. Use common courtesy. Don't park your boat on the ramp while retrieving your tow vehicle. Park at

a dock or beach it off the ramp. Loading is basically a reversal of launching. Again, two methods can be used: power or non-power. Trailer position is important in both cases. If using power-on, the best tactic is to have the trailer in the water just enough that a little power is needed to get the boat in place. This settles the boat correctly on the bunks. If the trailer is too deep, the boat can float side to the side and, when you pull out, may have shifted off the center of the trailer.

If using powered method, center the boat on the trailer as you enter the bunks. This means approaching upwind or up current. Use steady but low power for a constant forward motion, if possible. Make sure you're not approaching too fast. Shifting out of gear lessens your steering ability, often causing the boat to twist or turn on the approach. Make sure there is enough water for prop clearance, and use as little power as possible to move the boat bow eye up to the winch stand.

If using a non-power approach, again the trailer should not be parked so deep in the water that the boat floats high off the trailer when in position. You will, however, need enough water that the boat can be pulled up in position by hand with the docking line, or in some cases with the winch rope.

BOAT DRIVING

Driving today's bass boats is easy, but requires skills and practice,

especially with the more powerful engines and faster boats. Boats do not drive like automobiles. When you turn the wheel on a car, the front of the automobile changes direction. When you turn the wheel on a boat the back end swings around.

Read the boat and engine owner's manuals and familiarize yourself with all the operations. The first step is to make sure the boat is set up properly. A boat with the engine set at the wrong height, poorly centered on the transom, or a boat with the wrong prop can make a major difference in how a boat handles. Different hulls also perform differently. Don't expect to climb into a strange boat and immediately drive it wide open.

Regardless of whether you are a beginner at driving a bass boat, or driving a strange boat, begin driving at a comfortable speed that allows you to learn how to start, slow, stop, and turn the boat comfortably. Make turns in a variety of water conditions. Make stops so you can see how fast the boat moves through the water after you shut the engine down. Practice backing. As you gain confidence and gain a feel for the boat, you can gradually up the speed and attempt different maneuvers.

Most bass boats have hydraulic trim and tilt, located on the throttle control. When you first start to take off, the motor should be tucked all the way down against the transom. Increase throttle to power out of the hole. The front

Bass boats are fast and prospective operators should learn how to drive by starting at slow speeds and working up to faster speeds.

of the boat will climb up. Once the bow starts to settle back down, begin trimming up or raising the motor slowly. As you trim up, you will feel a "sweet spot" when the motor is trimmed correctly. The steering torque will almost vanish and the boat will ride smoothly over the water. At this point a bass boat should be riding on the rear pad alone. If you over-trim the boat – raise the motor too high – the boat will begin to rock from side to side (chine walk). If this happens, lower the motor slightly to get the bow back down.

DOCKING

Docking is the moment of truth for many boaters. If you blow it, your boat and your pride can get scarred simultaneously. And, it can even happen to the experts. Last

summer I came into a dock in heavy waves and just as I was docking, the bow of my boat went down, the dock went up and I sheared off the skeg of a very expensive trolling motor. Docking takes practice, but here are a few tips:

With the wind or current coming at you, approach with the boat bow slightly pointed in toward the dock with your stern at a slight angle away from the dock. As you near the dock, shift to neutral and let the boat's momentum carry you to the dock. Finally, just before the bow touches the dock, swing the outboard engine so that its back end is pointed toward the dock and give the engine a touch of reverse. This last maneuver, which admittedly takes some practice, will pull the stern of the boat up to the dock.

If the wind or current is flowing against the dock, you can take advantage of nature to make your

landing. Approach the dock at a small angle and pull around parallel to it when you're about a boat width off, then drift in. Always make sure you have bow and stern lines accessible and ready before you make your dock approach.

HIGH-SPEED DRIVING

Bass boats are basically designed for high-speed operation, and most bass boat drivers want to use speed to get to the best fishing holes fast. Driving at high speeds does require skill and practice. The higher speeds are achieved by a combination of throttle control and motor trimming.

Theoretically, the higher the motor is trimmed, the faster the boat can go – within limits. Too high and you start to lose water intake, which can cause prop slip and other problems. Often a high

High speeds produced by overtrimming can result in chine walking, a potentially dangerous situation.

rooster tail from a speeding boat means over trimming. It's extremely important to keep an eye on water pressure and temperature when driving a fully trimmed-out boat.

As a boat tester I often push boats past their comfortable driving limits, which often means causing chine walk on many boats. Chine walk is caused by many factors, the major one being the balancing of the boat on the small surface of the running pad. With full trim you may have less than a foot of the boat contacting the water surface. Propeller torque, sloppy engine mounting, and loose steering can also contribute. I've driven fully trimmed boats at high speeds without any chine walk, and other boats begin to rock well before the upper end of the motor rpm range is reached. Every boat is different.

An expert boat driver can achieve higher speeds by a technique called "driving through the chine walk," but it takes practice. Practice in a place with no boat traffic, plenty of room to run. A mild chop will help the boat to acquire lift with less trimming out. The more lift, the faster the boat will go. Accelerate the boat gradually and trim it out until you begin to feel the chine walk. Once oscillation of the stern begins, slightly turn the steering wheel to the right to counteract the left-turning forces of the prop torque. As you begin the slight turn to the right, gradually increase throttle and trim. If the oscillations increase, do not back off on the throttle, but trim down slightly until they stop and you feel you have the boat in control again.

Once you feel you're back in control, repeat the process, trimming out slightly and turning slightly to the left. If you continue this three-step sequence -- throttle, trim, left turn -- you can reach the top speed of the boat without oscillation. Once you learn these basic steps, you can eventually learn to counteract the oscillation with a very quick but slightly right turn of the steering wheel, snap it back and continue on a straight-line course, without undue chine walking. Some boats, however, simply can't be driven at high speeds without continuing this "hard-driving" technique. Proper or improper trimming can have other effects as well. Many beginning bass boat drivers tend to over trim. This can actually cause a drop in speed and an increase in engine rpm. Under trimming, especially at slower speeds, can cause the boat to "porpoise" – the bow rises and falls annoyingly. In both cases, simply trimming back down slightly will stop the problem.

Improper trimming can also cause problems on turns. Over trimming causes the boat to bounce and creates hard and dangerous handling problems. Under trimming, however, can also cause a dangerous handling problem on turns when the bow digs in. This can actually cause the boat to "hook," or spin on its axis.

BOATING SAFETY

According to a pamphlet by the United States Safe Boating Institute, over 1,000 people die in boating accidents every year. Nine out of ten of them drown. About half of those deaths involve alcohol. It's a tragic fact and not a joke, that 50 percent of drunk men who drown have their fly unzipped. Enough said?

When you're tipsy, you're much more likely to fall overboard. Alcohol also reduces your body's ability to protect against cold water. So within minutes you may not be able to call for help, or swim to safety. Actually, an intoxicated person whose head is immersed can be confused and swim down to death instead of up to safety. If that isn't enough to sober you up, consider that many states are now passing DUI laws for boaters. Being drunk on the water carries the same penalties as being drunk on the street!

You should also know how to safely operate your boat, and some states are considering passing boating safety tests. By law you are legally responsible for the safety of those on your boat as well as any damage your boat causes to others.

SAFE BOAT HANDLING

Several common-sense rules prevail. Powerboats must yield to sailboats and boats being rowed or paddled. In a narrow channel, this usually means coming off plane to a no-wake situation. You should also steer clear of all big vessels. As an observer several years ago at the Bassmaster Classic, my pro partner and I dropped over a barge wake, and the bass boat almost flipped over backwards.

The danger zone of any boat is from straight in front (the bow) to just past amidships of the right side. It's basically the same as when meeting another automobile at an intersection. The boat on the right has the right of way. You must yield to boats in that danger zone. When overtaking another boat, the lead boat always has the right of way. The boat being overtaken should stay on its side of the channel and maintain a steady speed so the overtaking boat can pass safely. When two boats meet head-on, or nearly so, as in a car, both should pass to the right and as far apart as practical, so it is easier and safer to cross each other's wake. It is okay to steer to the left if both boats know the plan. You can give notice by steering to the right or left while still far apart. Then stay with your plan unless the other boat does otherwise.

Inland boating rules are used throughout the country, and horn or whistle signals are used to indicate direction of travel. One short blast from either boat – which must be answered by the other boat – signals the intention to pass on the right, or port to port. Two short blasts indicate passing starboard to starboard. At night, running lights provide the information. Boats must have a green light on the starboard side, a red light on the port side and a white stern light that is visible 360 degrees. If you see a red light, you must stop and give way, because the other boat is passing to your right and has the right of way.

Avoid shipping channels, if possible, and cross them quickly when you must. Very few small boats survive collisions with ships. Learn to use charts and maps, and use up-to-date navigation charts. Understand the federal aids to navigation, or federal waterway marking system. Remember the old seafaring term "red right returning," which means the red buoys always mark the right of the channel when returning from open sea or going upstream in a river. Listen to VHF radio Channel 16. Make sure your lights are working properly and that you can be seen at night. Learn the proper whistle signals. Five or more blasts indicate trouble. Last, simply stay alert for dangers such as ships, barge traffic, underwater obstacles and other boaters, skiers, etc.

Safety Equipment

An important factor in safe boating is having the proper safety equipment aboard and making sure it's in working order.

1. Make sure you have the necessary equipment onboard to meet your state and federal requirements.
2. In fact, it's a good idea to contact your local water patrol office for a safety check. If you do this you may avoid being stopped and inspected when you're right in the middle of a hot fishing streak.
3. In addition to the correct number and type of PFDs, you generally need a fire extinguisher (one B-I type Coast Guard approved for boats 16 feet but under 26 feet).

4. Proper light displays are required to be shown from sunset to sunrise.
5. Boats carrying or using inflammable or toxic fluid such as gasoline must have efficient natural or mechanical ventilation systems.
6. A sounding device, either mouth, hand or power operated, that is audible for at least one-half mile is also required.
7. If operating in coastal waters, the Great Lakes, or the high seas, a visual distress signal is also required. The Skyblazer XLT aerial flare is a self-contained, hand-launched unit. Because no additional gun or launching mechanism is required, it's simple and launches up to 500 feet

altitude, burns for 8 seconds and floats in the water, making it accessible in a sinking or other life-threatening emergency.
8. In addition to these items, I would also suggest several others, including a first-aid kit, such as the soft-pack model from Sawyer.
9. A marine or CB radio is also invaluable.
10. Other potential lifesavers include extra fuses and a spare prop and prop nut. Denny Brauer even carries a spare trolling motor.
11. You should also have spare wire, terminal kit, socket and wrench set, pliers, a Phillips and a slot screwdriver, plus a roll of plastic electrician's tape.

A safe boating course is not a bad idea even for old salts. The United States Power Squadrons offer a boating course with the basics of safer and more enjoyable boating. All instruction is free. There is a nominal charge to cover costs, including a 150-page student workbook and chart. The course is offered as a public service in over 500 local areas throughout the U.S.A. The course is also available in video form. For information call: 1-800-828-3380. The United States Coast Guard Auxiliary, the Volunteer Civilian Arm of the United States Coast Guard, also teaches public boating courses and examines recreational boats for proper safety equipment. For more free information on boating safety (including safety recalls) call: 1-800-368-5647. Additional information on boating classes is available from United

Safe Boating Institute, 1504 Blue Ridge Road, Raleigh, NC 27622, 1-800-336-BOAT.

ROUGH WATER HANDLING

The best way to handle rough water is to avoid it. Learn to keep a weather eye out while on the water. Many knowledgeable boaters, including experts such as pro bass angler Denny Brauer monitor a weather channel on a weather radio.

But sometimes you simply can't avoid rough water, and you should learn to handle your boat in it. The first step is to say calm. Handling a boat in rough water can be scary, but it's not nearly as dangerous as you might think. The second step is to make sure everyone is wearing correctly fastened life jackets. Rain jack-

ets will also keep out cold rain and make a wet ride less miserable. Rain jackets are a good idea even if the sky is clear but the waves high. Place all passengers in the center of the boat and as low as possible. Secure everything in your boat, move coolers and other heavy gear forward for more control, and trim your motor down, then head for shore.

Rough water can be anything from a heavy chop to high waves and swells. The tactic and speed to handle them depends on the water conditions. For instance, in mild to medium chop – waves fairly close together – most expert boaters maintain a slightly high bow and a fairly high speed, or just enough to "ride" the waves without undue bouncing. If the ride gets too hard, try taking the waves at a slight angle of about 15 degrees. You'll get wet but come in home fast and safe. Like fishing and letting the bass tell you what they want on a particular day, you'll have to let the waves tell you the proper speed.

The speed problem occurs in high waves. When attempting to speed through heavy waves, the bow of the boat can be "stuffed" into a wave, driving the bow down under the wave and swamping the boat. To avoid such a situation you must be able to read the waves and maintain just enough speed to stay on top, instead of leapfrogging over one wave and into the next. This "surfing" tactic is accomplished by adding power going up the wave, to keep forward momentum, then reducing power on the down side, to prevent going so fast you punch into the incoming wave.

Another problem occurs here. Get three or so big waves coming almost on top of themselves, and the boat can literally be stopped and almost stood on its transom. That's where you need extra power to muscle up over the waves, and the reason for larger-horsepower motors.

Head into the waves, or quarter across them, if possible, even if it means the long way home. It's extremely important not to have a wave hit you broadside or from the stern. Running along the shoreline is not necessarily the safest, because shallow water tends to create more wave action. A good knowledge of the lake is also important, as you can sometimes make a short run to a less windy area, even if you have to make a longer run to your put-in.

Sometimes you will simply have to run broadside. It's a rough ride, but can be done with expert boat handling. The method is to tack across the troughs in a zigzag course instead of running parallel to the waves. First head into the waves at a 45-degree angle then make a 90-degree turn to ride with the sea. If the turn is made quickly, your boat will be broadside to the waves for only seconds. Tacking across the troughs is much safer than running broad-

side. It may take longer, but the chances of getting home safe are greatly increased.

Swells usually roll gently along, with well-rounded tops. They may be large, but the typical pleasure boat can handle swells fairly easily due to their rounded shape. If the swells become increasingly high, however, watch for a change in weather directions. When the sea becomes choppy due to the wind blowing at a 90-degree angle to the swells, things can indeed get rough.

Chapter 14

Rigging Tips from the Pros

Professional bass anglers, who literally live out of their boats, have very definite ideas about boats and how to rig them. Following are several of the top professional bass anglers and the boats they drive, as well as the motors, props, electronics and other gear they chose. Also included is information on whether they use a hotfoot, fixed or hydraulic jackplate and the battery systems they favor.

PENNY BERRYMAN

Boat: Nitro 929
Length: 21'2"
Motor: Mercury 225 OptiMax
Prop: 26 Tempest
Jackplate: Standard, 6-inch offset, fixed
Hotfoot: No. I ran a hotfoot one year, but I'm kind of short and the boat is big. I happened to be back in a stump field and I just needed to stand up a little to see ahead as I idled. Every time I tried to stand up, my foot came off the pedal. In extremely rough water I tend to lift up a little bit to take some of the impact off my back and use my knees to take some of the impact. When I did that of course my foot came off the hotfoot again. With a hotfoot you really have to keep your foot hard on the pedal.
Trim Control: On throttle
Steering: Hydraulic
Trolling Motor: MotorGuide 782 Tour Edition 36 volt, extra long shaft, 47 inches.
Electronics: Zercom LPG 2000 on bow identical units front and console with Humminbird NS25 gps.
Flasher/Temp: Zercom in-dash flasher
Sensor: I have always had the bow sensor mounted on trolling motor. The console unit sensor is mounted mid boat in sump area, not transom mounted
Batteries & System: 36 volt
Rigging Tips: A few years ago I asked Nitro to split the right hand rod box. They made me a custom deck with a split rod box. If you need more space, you don't have to move all your rods out of the way. You can use part of it for tackle or just be able to lift a part of the lid because when you're fishing, the lid is covered with rods.

I also had Nitro put in little dump trays on the floor of the boat to put spare crankbaits, etc. Just lay them right in the floor deck and they ride real safe, yet the lures are right at your fingertips. Plus, if you cut one off, it doesn't fly in your face as you're driving down the lake at 70 mph. It was this neat little holder. Now Nitro incorporates these lure holders, they've got two of them in every 9 series boat. They put a lot of thoughtfulness in the boats.

In the past you busted your knuckles or fingernails getting the hatch lids up. Nitro took the fiberglass and curved it in under the lid so now all you have to do is gently lift and your lid will easily come up.

CHAD & DENNY BRAUER

Boat: Ranger 520 VX
Length: 20' 9"
Motor: Evinrude 225 HO
Prop: 26 Raker
Jackplate: CMC 5" hydraulic, controlled from dash automatically.
Hotfoot: No
Trim Control: On throttle
Steering: Hydraulic
Trolling Motor: Minn Kota 101
Electronics: Zircom LPG-2000 on bow; Humminbird N525 with gps on console; Teleflex flasher on bow.
Flasher/Temp: Humminbird

in-dash flasher

Sensor: One internal mounted sensor

Batteries & System: 36-volt, Dual Pro batteries, lightning series

Rigging Tips: I used to keep a spare trolling motor, but I quit because the trolling motor I'm running has never had a malfunction plus it's the type of trolling motor that would be hard to change out very easily. The Ranger boats come rigged from the factory well enough that you really don't have to do anything. I do have Ranger mount my trolling foot pedal into the floor because of my bad back. This way I'm standing more level and have less strain on my back.

MARK DAVIS

Boat: Bass Cat Cougar
Length: 90'
Motor: 225 Mercury OptiMax
Prop: 26 Tempest
Jackplate: CMC, fixed
Hotfoot: Yes
Trim Control: Steering column
Steering: Hydraulic
Trolling Motor: Minn Kota 101
Electronics: Lowrance 1240A's bow and console; X15 with gps on console
Flasher/Temp: Bow and console
Sensor: Glassed in
Batteries & System: 36-volt
Rigging Tips: I don,t do a whole lot, I like to use the bow protector, that's not performance, but it sure helps. I don't do much special, just the normal stuff, make sure it is propped out right. Hole shot is my number one thing and then being able to lift the boat at low speeds is really important to me and that's all in the prop and transom. The reason I like to be able to lift my boat at low speeds is when you get in rough water, you can raise that bow up and that makes it a lot easier to get around. Speed is a big concern, but my main concern is being able to lift the boat at the lower speeds.

WOO DAVES

Boat: 929 Nitro
Length: 20' 9"
Motor: 225 Mercury OptiMax
Prop: Mercury Tempest 24 pitch
Jackplate: Hydraulic
Hotfoot: No
Trim Control: On throttle
Steering: Hydraulic
Trolling Motor: 36V MotorGuide Pro Model
Electronics: Raymarine 1470 fish finder on bow; C750 on console; RN300 gps
Flasher/Temp: Dash-mounted standard with Nitro
Sensor: Glassed in
Batteries & System: 36 volt
Rigging Tips: I usually wire my depth finder directly to the battery. I don't use the wiring harness, I wire it direct. I also always have a keel guard added to my boats. I usually mount a Gator Grip measuring board right in the floor in the center up next to that wall. One reason is you don't have to loan it to anybody and take a chance on not getting it back and two, it makes you measure your fish in the bottom of the boat. Plus it is out of the way and you know where it's at all the time.

I also use a Plano 14250 water-sealable tackle box to put tools in to keep them dry. That way your tools won't be rusted when you need them.

SHAW GRIGSBY
Boat: Triton TR20
Length: 20'
Motor: Mercury 225 OptiMax
Prop: 25 Tempest II
Jackplate: Bob's Machine,
6" hydraulic

Hotfoot: Yes
Trim & Jackplate Control:
Turn-signal style on steering
column
Steering: Hydraulic
Trolling Motor: MotorGuide,
109 Tour Edition
Electronics: Lowrance X15MT
with sonar, gps on console;
Lowrance X85 on bow
Flasher/Temp: In-dash flasher
standard with boat
Sensor: Glassed in
Batteries & System: 36 V
Rigging Tips: I do my own
custom rod straps, but there is
nothing to it. I pretty much
fish the boat as it comes from
the factory. I don't do anything
special.

ALTON JONES
Boat: Skeeter ZX225
Length: 20'2"
Motor: Yamaha 225
Prop: Yamaha Pro Series,
14, x 25 pitch
Jackplate: Standard Skeeter 12"
fixed

Hotfoot: Yes
Trim Control: Steering column
turn indicator type
Steering: Hydraulic
Trolling Motor: Minn Kota
Maxxum, 101 lbs., 36-volt
Electronics: Console, Lowrance
LCX 15 MT with complete
gps mapping; front, Lowrance
X91
Flasher/Temp: Lowrance
1240A Flasher; temps are front
and bow, included in the LCX
15 and X91
Sensor: Glassed in the rear
Batteries & System: 36 volt
system
Rigging Tips: I prefer to mount
all my electronics myself as
opposed to having it done,
because instead of using wood
screws and mounting it to the
console, I like to thru-bolt
everything with stainless steel
washers and stop nuts. Because
we are often in such severe
rough conditions, I want to

totally bullet-proof them and
make sure there is no chance of
anything coming loose. I also
like to sit in the boat and make
sure the screens are angled to
where I'm going to be sitting
to get the best possible viewing
angles. I do all my own set-up
as far as jackplate height, prop
selection and all that sort of
thing to optimize performance.

I think the most important
thing as far as making the boat
run at the peak of its performance curve is to load the boat
fully just as you would during a
tournament before you do the
set-up. So many guys get a
brand-new boat and set it up
for top speed with maybe 10
gallons of gas, no fishing equipment and one person and then
they wonder why when they
load it down on tournament
day that it doesn't run like it is
supposed to. Do the set-up
with the weight in the boat
that you expect to have in the
tournaments. It's not uncom-
mon for someone to outrun
me on practice day when I'm
by myself, have a light load and
no fish in the livewell, but you
get me out there against the
same boat the next morning
with a full load and I'm going
to blow right past him when it
counts.

GARY KLEIN
Boat: Triton TR20
Length: 20'
Motor: Mercury 225 EFI
Prop: Mercury 26 pitch, 3-blade
Jackplate: Detwiller 6" hydraulic
Hotfoot: Yes
Trim & Jackplate Control:
On steering column

Steering: Hydraulic, Land & Sea, standard on Triton

Trolling Motor: MotorGuide 36 V. I carry a spare trolling motor and prop.

Electronics: Zircom flasher, LCF40's, real time

Flasher/Temp: Temp Zircom; flasher temp SID

Sensor: Glassed in.

Batteries & System: 36 volt, Dual Pro Magnum, group 31 totally maintenance free

Rigging Tips: Detwiller has a dial switch which I eliminate. I put a manual switch that resembles a turn signal on the steering column. The dial is the only trouble I've heard anybody has had with a Detwiller. The numbers on the dial are not important to the boat driver, I don't care if it's set on 2 or 3, 4 or 5, you drive a boat by feel. Most positions where the dial is placed you can't read the dial anyway, so it doesn't mean a thing.

I'm probably the most basic on boat rigging of any fishermen on the circuit. I am adamant about my boat being my office and everything within that area should be second nature to me. I've often said the fish are conditioned by their environment, hot and cold, etc., well the angler is also conditioned by his environment. The only difference is that we have total control on how we want to condition ourselves. I've always had a thing, my entire career, that I push things up the flagpole until I have all the answers. Once I figure something out, I never have to go down that road again. I,ve already done all my research in that area and I know that this is the best knot to tie and this is the best hook to use or these are the best action fishing rods or this is the best way to rig a boat. You can talk boats, motors, jackplates, battery systems, depth finders, but once I get something right, I never change. Every boat I rig is identical. The only difference may be a color change. Every switch, every dial in my last year's boat or in the previous year's boat is exactly the same as I have in my boat now. My performance is based on what I weigh in and the decisions I make on the water. And a lot of the way a boat is rigged has to be almost like an extension of me. It,s just like the techniques and the fishing rods, we do it so often that it,s just a flow and it is the same thing with a boat, it has to be correctly put together, because there are a lot of situations you get into that call for a reaction. If you're in a boat with a piece of equipment you're not familiar with, then you're not able to make the right reaction.

LARRY NIXON

Boat: Stratos 21

Length: 21'

Motor: Evinrude 225

Prop: Raker 26

Jackplate: Fixed

Hotfoot: No

Trim Control: On throttle

Steering: Hydraulic

Trolling Motor: Minn Kota 74

Electronics: Lowrance 160 GPS on console; Lowrance 1240A and Eagle X65 on bow

Flasher/Temp: Flasher in units in-dash and bow

Sensor: Glassed in

Batteries & System: 24 volt

Rigging Tips: I do a lot of little things just to make sure things stay intact for the whole season. I tie everything together with tie straps, double check everything to make sure my boat is rigged out to take the rigors of tournament fishing. I mount my spare prop in the back portion of the boat so that it,s buckled down good and solid and not bouncing around all the time. I put what I call a bounce-buster on my trolling motor so it doesn't wear out during the course of the year and I also put a strap around the shaft.

KEVIN VANDAM

Boat: Nitro 929 CDX
Length: 20' 9"
Motor: 225 Mercury OptiMax
Prop: 25 Tempest
Jackplate: Bob's High
  Performance Hydraulic
Hotfoot: Yes
Trim & Jackplate Control:
  Turn-signal style lever mounted
  on the steering column con-
  trols both units.
Steering: Hydraulic, SeaStar
Trolling Motor: MotorGuide
  109, Pinpoint Ready, Tour
  Edition
Electronics: Pinpoint 7420 on
  the bow with the trolling
  motor; Pinpoint 7520 with gps
  on the console.
Flasher/Temp: Yes, but I don't
  use the flasher. Temperature is
  on both sonars.
Sensor: Mounted on the transom.
Batteries & System: I run a 36
  volt, three-battery system and
  use a Stealth battery management system. It's a plug-in
  charger and also takes voltage
  from your engine. Once your
  cranking battery is charged, it
  transfers the power to your
  trolling motor batteries.
Rigging Tips: To me, everything
  on the bass boat is very important. I rig my own and I've
  learned over the years, placement in the boat, everything
  you see and even things you
  don't see, is important. For

instance, which side your batteries, the battery charger and all
that is located really is critical as
far as weight and balance to optimize your performance. If you
put a battery on one side, you
need to have a battery on the
opposite side to balance out
your boat.

You also need to think of
what things weigh, not only
before you store or mount them
in your boat, but with an
emphasis on how you use them.
Electronics placement for example. Trolling motor, rod tie
downs, I'm real picky about all
that.

I'm real particular about a lot
of little things. For instance the
measuring board. My bump stick
is screwed to the floor right
behind where the front deck
drops down because I remember
when I saw a 12-incher get away
from another angler during the
Classic and with that fish he
might have won. I prefer the little rubber tie-downs for rod
straps. A lot of companies are
now using retractable rod straps,
but I still prefer the T & H
Marine little rubber jobs because
they don't fray your line or catch
crankbait hooks. I install those
myself including one for my
partner in the back.

They put tackle management
systems and rod holders in the
boats these days, but I remove
those or move them around so I
can stick more rods in the box.
With a tube system the box
might hold 15 rods, but the space
is big enough to hold 25 rods.

MIKE WURM

Boat: Ranger 520 Comanche,
  single console
Length: 21'6"
Motor: Yamaha 225 VMAX
Prop: 25 Yamaha
Jackplate: Rite Hite, 6" fixed
Hotfoot: Yes
Trim Control: Column
Steering: Hydraulic
Trolling Motor: MotorGuide
  109, 36 volt
Electronics: Raymarine L470
  on bow; L755 with gps, on
  console
Flasher/Temp: included in
  Raymarine units
Sensor: Glassed in.
Batteries & System: 36 volt
Rigging Tips: I still like to put
  my transducer on the foot of
  the trolling motor on the bow.
  It gives me a direct signal
  without going through the
  boat. I always have an extra
  bilge pump installed when I
  order the boat. Other than that
  I don't do anything special.